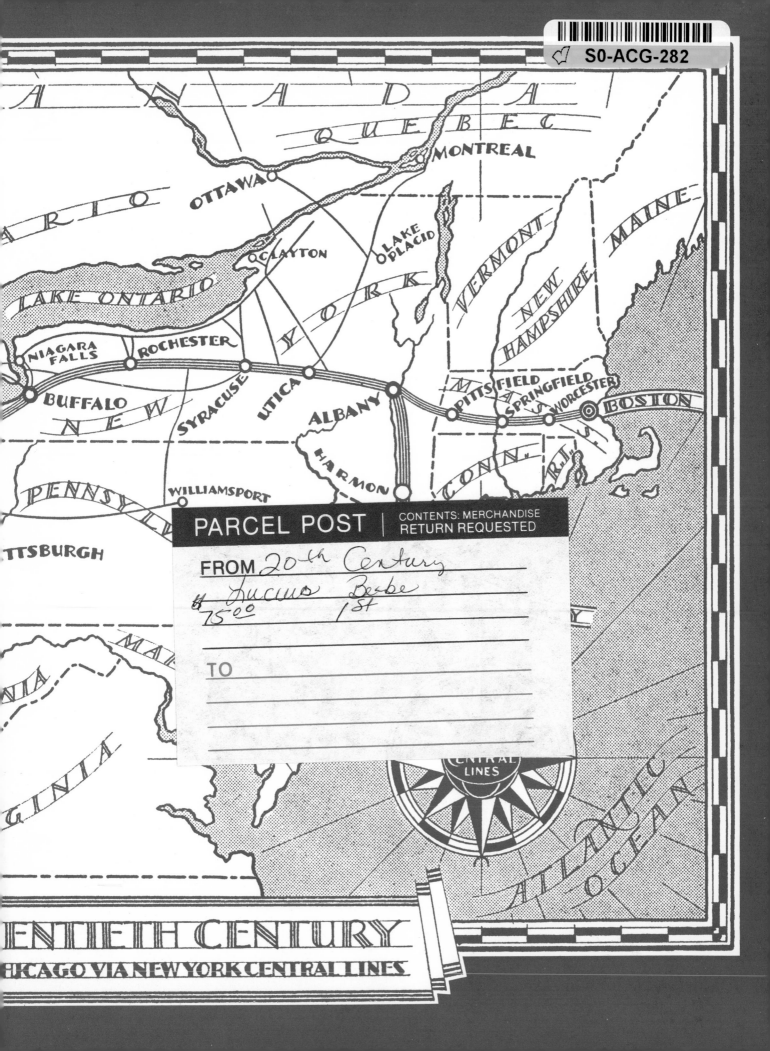

PARCEL POST | CONTENTS: MERCHANDISE
RETURN REQUESTED

FROM 20th Century
Lucius Beebe
$75.00 1st

TO

CENTRAL
LINES

TWENTIETH CENTURY
CHICAGO VIA NEW YORK CENTRAL LINES

"THE GREATEST TRAIN IN THE WORLD"

20TH CENTURY

By ★

Lucius Beebe

HOWELL-NORTH - 1962 - BERKELEY, CALIFORNIA

TWENTIETH CENTURY

Printed and bound in the United States of America.
Library of Congress Catalogue Card No. 62-17074.

ISBN 0-8310-7031-5

1st printing March, 1962
2nd printing July, 1962
3rd printing September, 1962
4th printing April, 1964
5th printing November, 1966
6th printing August, 1967
7th printing February, 1970

Published by Howell-North Books
1050 Parker Street, Berkeley, California 94710

Frontispiece: *Red Carpet at Grand Central* by Stan Repp.

Acknowledgments

For their generous assistance in the form of editorial and picture material for the preparation of this book the author is indebted to a number of collaborators, some of them within the framework of the railroad industry, others among the amateurs of its not altogether departed wonderments. They include the ever helpful Everett De Golyer of Dallas, curator of what is perhaps the most extensive and authoritative iconography of the American railroading scene, President John Barriger of the Pittsburgh & Lake Erie Railroad, photographers Edward L. Mays, John P. Ahrens, Jim Shaughnessy and H. W. Pontin of Rail Photo Service, Richard Maney, who once publicized the run of the play "Twentieth Century" and Phillip Dunning who staged it, Edward Lehman of W. H. Miner, Inc., of Chicago, for permission to reproduce the Howard Fogg jacket illustration, Nora Wilson of Pullman Standard, May Seymour of The Museum of the City of New York, photographer Jesse E. Hartman, Abe Smith, Superintendent of New York Central Dining Car Services, Rogers Whitaker, E. B. White for permission to reprint his poem "The Twentieth Century Gets Through," Bennett Cerf, Merle Armitage, D. E. Motlow of Jack Daniels, Norman Rockwell and the Curtis Publishing Company, Henry Sell of *Town & Country*, William I. Nichols, John O'Hara, Harry Hansen, Alfred Lunt and Gloria Swanson for reminiscences and anecdotal material concerning *The Century*, and Stan Repp for the fine painting that is the combined title page and frontispiece. And over and above all others, be they howsoever generous and knowledgeable, he is in debt to ANN KUSS of the publicity department of the New York Central railroad whose enthusiasm for the project and whose participation in its every detail must elevate her to the status of a partner in whatever recognition this book may achieve.

To

John Barriger

President of The Pittsburgh & Lake Erie Railroad
Whose Devotion to the History, Folklore
and Iconography of Railroading Identify
Him as an Unique Executive Who Is Also
a Scholar and Patron of the Arts Who
Recognizes No Distinction Between Work
and Pleasure, This Book Is Dedicated.

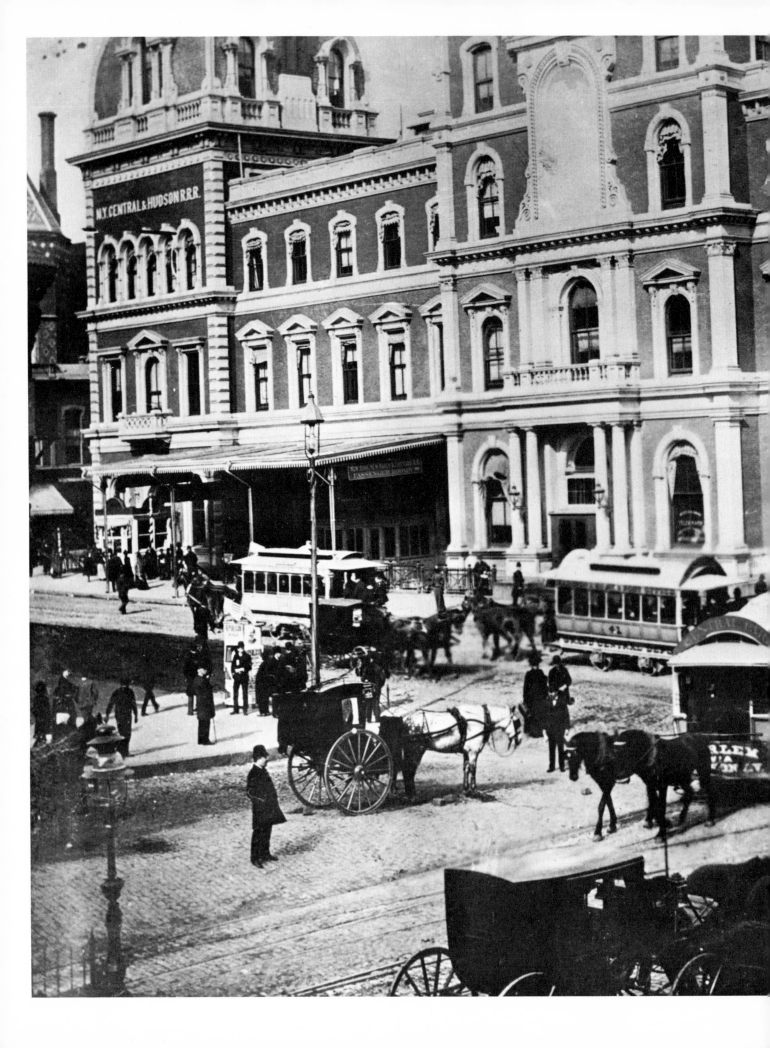

Contents

Foreword

Ships and hotels, it must be obvious, have enjoyed over the years an ample bibliography. They are the abodes of wonderment and romance, the tents of opulence where takes his one night's rest the sultan of the "Rubaiyat". Their sailing lists and registers have been the roll call of names that make news and the rich fabric of their being lends itself almost inescapably to the student of times and places, manners and people because here they are on parade the way the great of the world always should be.

Monographic portraits have been devoted to such hostelries of legend as the Savoy, the Adlon, the Waldorf Astoria, the Brown Palace in Denver, Parker's in Boston, The Palace in San Francisco and the Paris Ritz. Their properties of opulence have fired the imagination and they have appeared thinly disguised or not at all in fiction and the drama, the Savoy in Arnold Bennett's "Hotel Imperial" and The Adlon in Vicki Baum's "Grand Hotel". Specific hotels have been evoked in individual scenes in dramas beyond tally, but one cannot but recall the magnificence of the Adam foyer of the New York Ritz Carlton in which Ethel Barrymore died so stylishly in Brock Pemberton's production in 1919 of "Declassée".

Ships of adventure, discovery and especially vessels of war have been immortalized between boards also beyond convenient listing and full book treatment has been accorded to such luxury liners as *Titanic, Morro Castle, Queen Mary, Paris* and *United States*. The exalted status of their patrons, the splendor of the engineering and appointments and in the case of *Titanic,* the incredible melodrama of its end, have made them almost unavoidable objects of literary attention. Walter Lord's "A Night To Remember" found its mystical companion piece in James Gould Cozzens' novella, "S. S. San Pedro" which is an only thinly veiled and parallel account of the ill-fated *Vestris*.

In the realm of railroading, however, I can think of but a single train that enjoys the distinction of major, professional book treatment. It is the night train from Burntisland in "Disaster at Dundee" by John Prebble and even here the doomed steamcars play a secondary role to the starred villainy of the great Tay Bridge which destroyed them and all they carried.

Writers of novels, drama and screen scenarios have been quick to perceive the explicit romance of railroad travel, and the resulting bibliography of trains as vehicles or incidental properties of fiction and the stage is immense. In recent years filmgoers have ridden vicariously to adventure aboard "Union Pacific," "Shanghai Express" and "The Harvey Girls," "Dodge City," "42nd Street," "North by Northwest," and it is significant that the first of all films with a discernible plot was "The Great Train Robbery." Novels beyond number have emplaced their protagonists in the staterooms, compartments, club cars, diners and lounges of the universal train. Two geographic regions over all others seem to have produced trains where melodrama was the most essential element of their cargo: the Carpathians and the French Riviera. Adventurers, spies, international agents, merchants of death and king's messengers swarmed on the *Simplon-Orient Express* almost to the exclusion of casual tourists, salesmen and commercial travelers, and it may be conjectured that the late E. Phillips Oppenheim, the past master of fictional elegance, couldn't have made a living without *The Blue Train* between Paris and Monte Carlo. Here in compartments bristling with orchids, silver wine coolers, Vuiton luggage (an absolute essential to top drawer travel), sable bedthrows, six litre firkins of caviar and jeweled traveling clocks from Cartier, rode the elect of earth, monocled, morning coated, silk hatted and gowned by Worth amidst grand dukes, monarchs incognito, emissaries of the Czar, Greek multimillionaires and Balkan munitions merchants. They were plied with costly and exotic viands and sluiced with rare vintages by obsequious lackeys in the knee breeches, tailcoats and silk stockings of the *Compagnie des Wagons Lits et Grand Express Européans,* coded messages were taken on and dispatched at every operations stop, tiaras gleamed in the restaurant car and, of course, everyone dressed for dinner.

And all this had its factual counterpart in real life aboard the luxury trains of a prewar Europe, traces of which survive to this very day among the only slightly faded salons of *The Blue Train*.

Generally speaking these upholstered accessories of *ton* obtained in American railroad travel only in the private cars of the well-to-do where they flourished in luxurious profusion, and train travel available to the public has been characterized by a more republican simplicity. There are, however, in the record American trains maintained at such a degree of excellence as to compare favorably in their appointments and conduct with the best Europe or England had to offer.

Foremost among these in celebrity was *The Twentieth Century Limited*. For well over five decades it was so well regarded that nobody, save possibly the competing Pennsylvania Railroad which maintained the rival *Broadway Limited* took exception to its boast of being "The Greatest Train in The World" any more than anyone has ever questioned the similar claim of Rolls Royce to being "The Finest Car in The World."

The Twentieth Century Limited was simply the established standard of speed, comfort and reliability to which all others were compared and its sailing lists were the names that made news everywhere, the people one encountered aboard *The Mauretania*, in the Via Mizner at Palm Beach, in the bar of the Paris Ritz or at Claridge's in London.

Far from being a train of Byzantine lavishness, *The Century* was throughout its glory years a rather austere arrangement as trains went. It didn't charge a $25. surcharge and run once a week while presenting its women passengers with orchids and men with alligator billfolds as did the Santa Fe's *De Luxe*. Its menus couldn't compare with the Fred Harvey opulence of quail in aspic or the Bal-timore & Ohio's terrapin. It didn't advertise rhumba bands and dance floors as some of the seasonal Florida trains did in the twenties. Its bar cars were less conducive to rich disorders among the bottles than the oases aboard the Illinois Central's *Panama Limited*.

Essentially *The Century* was a Vanderbilt train. It rode over a Vanderbilt network of affiliated railroads, it came into being at a time when the Vanderbilt dynasty still ruled the destinies of the New York Central and even its details had implications of Vanderbilt excellence. The butter on its dining cars came from the Vermont dairy farm of a Vanderbilt in-law.

The Century was patronized by people who took the best of everything for granted, who put up at the Blackstone or St. Regis at either end of its run, whose wine and cigars derived from Park & Tilford, clothes from Henry Poole and letters of credit were drawn against Morgan Harjes in Paris. It was an explicit evidence of well-being to ride it like being seated at Sir James Charles' table on the *Aquitania* and having credit at Tiffany's. At the beginning of its run its patronage derived from the pages of Gertrude Atherton. By the thirties it was out of John O'Hara.

Of it the novelist Michael Arlen once remarked: "I take *The Century* because I want very little in this world, only the best and there's so little of that."

It was in the spirit of Arlen's philosophy that *The Twentieth Century Limited* was operated in its golden noontide, and it is in the same spirit that this enquiry into its character and being is conducted.

Lucius Beebe

Virginia City
1962

FOUR TRACKS ALONG THE HUDSON

It is the dawn of a fine spring day late in May and let us say in the year 1934, take or add a page of the calendar, for the scene we are asked to conjure up in the mind's eye of remembrance lasted for a decade backward and another decade forward into the unforeseeable forties. The viewer is invited to envision over the years and from a vantage point on the Hudson at Manitou or Peekskill the broad waters of the lordly river flecked with early morning shipping and the Jersey Palisades in the misty distance. In the foreground, gleaming and sinuous, are the four mainline tracks of the New York Central Railroad curving out of sight around a headland on their way to Albany or, if you prefer, Ultima Thule.

It is between five and six o'clock. In nearby Yonkers the milk is being delivered with sound effects of rattling containers and awakened dogs. Over the shoulder of the beholder, a few miles down the line toward the great city, a column of smoke and steam exhaust rises vertically to show where are the roundhouse and ready tracks at Harmon with their motive power in waiting. Over the tracks there is a hush of expectancy, for the great act of the day is about to begin, heralded by the chime whistle of a train somewhere around the headland in the direction of Garrison.

It is just five o'clock and around the bend, running fast under a curving banner of coal smoke that hangs stationary on the morning air, comes the first train of The Parade. It is No. 36, an undistinguished bread-and-cheese sleeper run called *The Genesee* with overnight Pullmans from Buffalo and Rochester, Oswego and Utica, and others from the Adirondack Division, Tupper Lake Junction and Lake Placid with head-end revenue cars to match. Because it is at the head of The Parade and must get in and out of Harmon ahead of its betters,

it is hurrying and rolls past in a long line of dark green cars with no observation platform to bring a panache to its passing, for it is a train of no great pedigree.

On its heels, ten minutes later, comes *The Iroquois,* Train No. 30, Pullmans only, deriving from Toronto, Buffalo and Rochester with others gathered in from the St. Lawrence Division, Watertown, Ogdensburg and Massena. *The Iroquois* has more class and boasts a club lounge but no diner for it, too, will be in Manhattan before breakfast time.

Following by a scant ten minutes margin comes Train No. X4, *The Fast Mail* with sleepers from Chicago, Cleveland, Niagara Falls and Buffalo, a lounge car all the way and a diner and parlor car on the upstate daylight hours of its run. It has ample head-end revenue, mail storage cars, Railway Post Office cars to justify its name, and wooden high cars of outmoded vintage showing the red and green diamond herald of Railway Express to gladden the hearts of accountants at 466 Lexington Avenue.

Right on the heels of *The Fast Mail* arrives a train with some suggestions of style in its going. It is *The Montreal Limited*, Pullmans only from Montreal to New York and a club car over the connecting Delaware & Hudson and behind it, with a matter of only moments to spare, comes its companion on the Montreal run, *The Mount Royal* with coaches and sleepers over the Rutland through deepest Vermont.

Next on the time card and clicking through like clockwork is a truly massive consist, No. 4, *The New York Special*. It has sleepers from Chicago, Detroit, Niagara Falls, Cleveland, Buffalo and Lockport, coaches, a diner, lounge car and buffet and 250 first class passengers are sleeping in its staterooms, drawing rooms and behind the still prevailing green cloth curtains of open sections. A flashing of synchronized side motion, a hail of cinders, a long drawn muted thunder of trucks over rail joints, and *The New York Special* has gone, leaving the stage set for the big event of the day.

This is the passage in glory of Train No. 26, *The Twentieth Century Limited*, all-Pullman extra fare flyer from Chicago to New York on the tightest schedule known, with deluxe standard Pullmans with drawing rooms, staterooms and compartments, single and double bedrooms, valet, barber and maid service. There is Porterhouse steak on the menu, fresh flowers on every table, a steward on bowing terms with the great of the great world, a conductor with a pink in his buttonhole and Pullman porters who are the *haute noblesse* of the social midst in which they move. The names on its sailing list are the names of headlines, and beside a passenger list of exalted dimensions, *The Century*, carries an intangible but equally glittering freight, the pride of a great operation and a tradition of complete excellence unmatched by any railroad in the world.

Showpiece, legend, article of railroad faith, *The Twentieth Century Limited* is a national institution, moving with the exactitude of sidereal time, as implacable as Fate. Its passage down the Valley of the Hudson every morning is the triumph of a proconsul, and from the pilot of its J-1 Hudson Type locomotive to the electric lit herald on its observation platform it is a matter of moment. People of diminished importance rode it to be associated with people of authentic stature in their various worlds. No guest list or passenger list anywhere, neither the register of The Palace Hotel in San Francisco nor that of the old *Mauretania* when she was the blue ribband vessel of the Atlantic sea lanes, boasted more effulgent celebrities. Women of fashion who lunched one day at the Pump Room and the next day at The Colony dined on *The Century* in between. Tycoons en route from a director's meeting in La Salle Street to a finance committee at the Bankers Club read *The Wall Street Journal* in the club car of *The Century*.

Actors en route from Broadway successes to long term contracts in Hollywood went between their destinations aboard *The Century* and its appropriate counterpart west of Chicago, *The Chief*, *The Super-Chief*, the *Los Angeles Limited* or *The Golden State*. In an earlier time they had taken *The California Limited* or the Santa Fe's *De Luxe*. On days when its arrival in Manhattan coincided with sailings of the *Olympic, Mauretania* or *Berengaria, The Century* was awash with international travelers with Vuiton luggage and the labels of the Crillon and Savoy hotels on their hatboxes. An older world of upper case security, wealth and importance flowed through the train gates at Grand Central and La Salle Street to the green Pullmans with the assurance of privacy and perfection once they mounted the steps of the world's premier train and the showpiece of the railroad industry. No breath of scandal rode *The Century*. Notoriety might be on the passenger list, but strict propriety characterized its stay as guest of the New York Central.

A man might get as drunk as a Roman proconsul in the club car if the whim was on him, and many a late night session at poker or bridge only broke up as the train was slowing for its terminal in the morning, but he might not make the acquaintance of a stranger and no introductions were performed on the cars by conductors, train secretaries or porters. There is no record of sleeping space issued for a single passenger being occupied by two. No well heeled salesman sent wine to single women in the diner.

In this climate of almost unearthly rectitude, *The Twentieth Century Limited* plied on its lawful occasions for a full fifty years of untarnished performance to become a great tradition of travel in a world in which travel was still conducted with something approximating style.

The century of Christian chronology for which it was named was two years old when *The Twentieth Century Limited* was born. A number of factors figured in the decision of the Central's management to place in operation a regularly scheduled winter and summer luxury train on the Chicago-New York run with a flat twenty hour carding between the two terminals.

The history of the train itself really went back to 1893, an epochal year in American railroading generally, when the World's Columbian Exposition at Chicago had proved at once the greatest showpiece and greatest incentive to rail travel in the history of the industry. The Transportation Exhibit was a fantastic drawing card with locomotives, cars and up-to-the-minute devices of every sort on view from engine and car builders, signal manufacturers and everyone interested in the industry that was then the greatest of all American preoccupations. From all points of the compass, too, the carriers converging on Chicago had spread themselves with name trains dedicated to the Fair itself and with special excursions, many of them of luxury dimensions and in cars especially built and equipped for the occasion. In Boston an enterprising carbuilder named G. E. Allen, Superintendent of the Old Colony Railroad, had designed and put into service over the Fitchburg Railroad and its connections a compartment car with all-room floor plans on which visitors to the Fair lived in the Chicago yards for the duration of a several-day visit. Knowing that his guests might well have swollen feet at the end of a long day's sightseeing on foot, he provided each compartment with a foot bath countersunk beneath the floor and concealed by a trap in which the tired tourist might soothe his aching joints in a nice hot soak.

From New York both the Central and the Pennsylvania had inaugurated fast de luxe trains to serve the Exposition, the Pennsylvania's being the *Pennsylvania Special,* direct forerunner of the later *Broadway Limited* and the Central's showpiece being called *The Exposition Flyer. The Flyer,* although it was withdrawn from the time card at the end of the Fair, had been on an incredible twenty-hour schedule, nine years before *The Century* was contemplated. In that time many improvements had been made and the Central's management decided that what had in 1893 been a temporary *tour de force,* in 1902 might well be placed in service on a permanent and practicable basis.

In that interval the Central's chief engineer, General William J. Wilgus, had inaugurated the first hundred pound six-inch high steel rail ever laid in the United States over long stretches of track. Grades had been reduced and curves eliminated and an over-all program of speeding up the carrier's traffic, both freight and passenger, had been promulgated. Improvements extended all along the operating line and included greatly advanced signal operation and communication of orders, heavier ballast had been laid on the roadbed, car design stepped up and the entire technique of train operations had reached a degree of precision and maturity.

Chief beneficiary of the improvements inaugurated by the Central in the nineties and after the turn of the century was the *Lake Shore Limited,* a magnificently appointed all-luxury equipped flyer between New York and Chicago with a Boston section which joined the main consist at Albany over the tracks of the Boston & Albany, which in 1900 was to become, by lease, part of the New York Central. The *Lake Shore,* in its time, had about it many of the overtones of elegance later to be assumed by *The Century.* Until 1899 when the Wagner firm of carbuilders went out of business to be absorbed by Pullman, all its sleepers, diners and club cars had been outshopped to specification for the *Lake Shore* and carried its insigne on their nameboards. Such fine sleepers and buffets as *Pinzon, Bracquemonde* and *Malacca* with their olive green liveries and the elaborately scrolled finelining that was a hallmark of Wagner manufacture became household names along the Water Level Route. The New York Central Lines had switched, perforce to Pullman after a quarter of a century's allegiance to Wagner, only three years before the *Twentieth Century Limited* was to make its first run.

The stage was set for a dramatic innovation, although the audience contained the usual number of skeptics. When the inaugural run of what was destined to become the most celebrated name train in the world was announced the management was immediately conscious of catcalls and other noises of derision from the wings.

"Surely it is only an experiment," wrote a British commentator of the time. "Can so high a rate of speed as will be necessary to accomplish the feat be maintained daily without injury to the engine, the rails and the coaches? The operators will soon find that they are wasting fortunes in keeping their property in condition, and then, loving money better than notoriety, the twenty-hour project will be abandoned."

American railroaders took scant stock in English concern for the wear and tear on their locomotives and recalled that three-quarters of a century earlier, when American roads were importing engines of British manufacture and the mechanics to operate them, the enginemen had refused to allow their locomotives to operate in wet weather.

Some properties and institutions become the stuff of legend over long periods of years, as witness such various repositories of folklore as John L. Sullivan, *The Boston Evening Transcript,* the Waldorf Astoria, the Hope Diamond, the Boardwalk at Atlantic City, Mrs. Potter Palmer, *Town Topics* and The Girl From Rectors, all of which were coeval with the beginnings of *The Twentieth Century Limited* and all of them characteristic of America in their time. It required the conscious or unconscious pyramiding of episodes of mythology, fact or contrivance over a period of time to establish these several entities in the American awareness and associate with them the qualities and attributes for which they were eventually celebrated.

The Twentieth Century (the *Limited* came five days later on June 20) was celebrated and institutional from the date of its first run. It may or may not be significant that the cornerstone of the enormous body of legend which was to gather around it was laid by John W. (Bet-A-Million)

Gates, a contemporary who was already and in his own right the central character in an untidy body of American folklore when he started *The Century* on its way. Gates, a vulgarian of the first chop who had made a substantial fortune in the manufacture of barbed wire and achieved worldwide notoriety for his gambling proclivities, was on the first sailing westbound and was so delighted with the experience that he turned around and returned to New York when *The Century* sailed that afternoon. Greeted at Chicago by the press, he remarked quotably enough that the train was destined to make New York a suburb of Chicago. In Manhattan he diplomatically told the reporters that *The Century* would inevitably make Chicago a suburb of New York.

If these sentiments didn't approach the wit as epigrams of, say, Oscar Wilde, their easy quotability made them immediately conversational currency in the men's bar at The Windsor Hotel in Fifth Avenue and the Palmer House barbershop on Lake Michigan, and they started *The Twentieth Century Limited* on a run in the American awareness of spectacular things that wasn't to slacken or be abated for fifty years.

BOSTON SECTION CLASSIC: *(Rail Photo Service: H. W. Pontin.)*

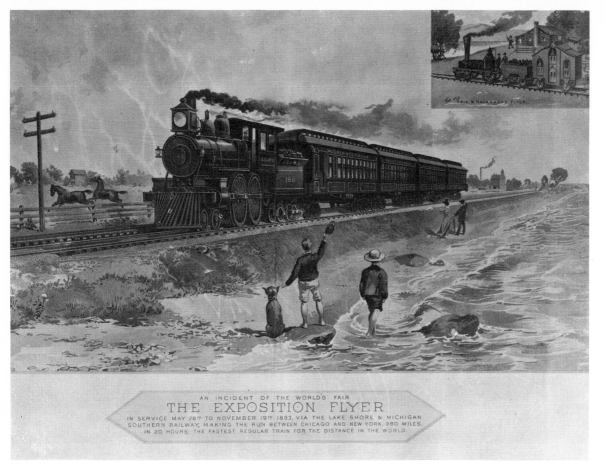

The train that inspired *The Twentieth Century Limited* and was the prototypal twenty-hour limited between New York and Chicago was *The Exposition Flyer* of 1893 placed in seasonal operation for the duration of the World's Columbian Exposition on the shore of Lake Michigan. As was to be true in the later *Century* and *The Twenty Hour Special*, later *The Broadway, The Exposition Flyer* was met by a competing Pennsylvania train on an identical schedule thus setting the precedent of meeting the opposition that was to last until the 1960s. The poster here reproduced shows *The Exposition Flyer* running over its Lake Shore & Michigan Southern trackage with an insert of "The Old Erie & Kalamazoo Flyer" with its steeple crowned passenger car for comparison. Below is one of the superb Wagner-built combination buffet-club-baggage cars which were standard equipment on all luxury runs on the Vanderbilt roads until the turn of the century. *(Above: New York Central; Below: Arthur D. Dubin Collection.)*

The Exposition Flyer of 1893 running here with six cars instead of the four Wagners of the poster view is shown along the Hudson, probably at Bear Mountain in this uncommonly rare action photograph. The American Standard 4-4-0 type locomotive on the head end and at the right was standard on such 1890 name trains as the *Empire State Express* and *Lake Shore Limited.* The above consist shows the ever-present Wagner buffet-combine on the head end, a Wagner parlor car, two Wagner sleepers and two coaches, perhaps deadheading from Albany, on the rear. *(Two Photos: Everett De Golyer Collection.)*

Here, on the morning of June 19, 1902 with Thomas Sherwood at the throttle and Thomas Jordan firing, the New York Central & Hudson River Railroad's No. 2960 powers the first run of Train No. 26, *The Twentieth Century Limited* eastbound between Albany and New York. In the diner Bet-a-Million Gates was having steak for breakfast and ranking officials were watching the mileposts and checking them against the new operating timecard. *The Century* was off for a date with destiny that was to endure for more than six decades. *(New York Central.)*

In 1902 when *The Century* was inaugurated, the quick lunch counter at Grand Central Terminal was a favorite with businessmen who had no time for the more elaborate ritual of Delmonico's which was only four blocks away or at Simeon Ford's Grand Union Hotel just across Forty-second Street. Then as in later years the pan fried oysters and cream lobster stew were favorites but the attire of gentle-men was more on the formal side and whiskers were abundant. The train shed *(below)* had changed little from the seventies except for raised platforms and new train gates, and *The Twentieth Century Limited* which left daily at 2:45 from Track 20. *(Above: Museum of the City of New York; Below: New York Central.)*

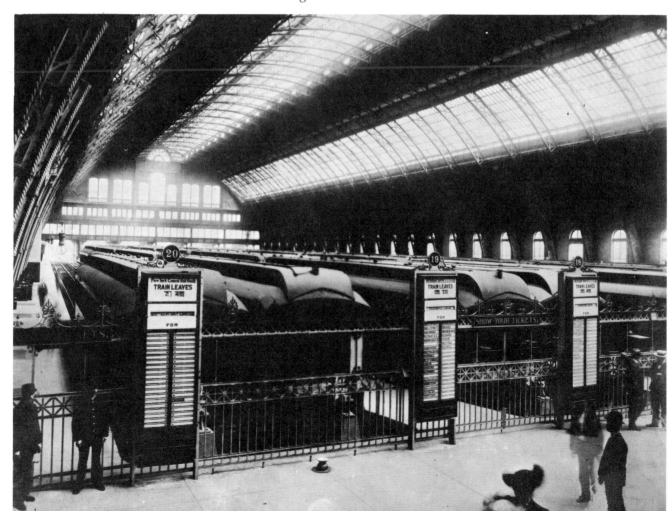

Europe was being engulfed in the opening battles of World War I when this picture of *The Century* with electric motive power was taken in September 1914 at Riverdale, New York, almost into Harmon. Below, probably for a publicity shot, *The Century* races an old-time steam inspection engine along the Hudson. *(Two Photos: Everett De Golyer Collection.)*

Racing *The Twentieth Century Limited* became a sort of universal index of speed and daring in other vehicles over the years because its reputation made it a standard of measurement for comparison. Speedboats raced it down the Hudson and primeval flying machines clattered beside it from Poughkeepsie to Harmon in tests of acceleration and endurance, but automobiles, lacking an adjacent highway on which to be photographed, sought competition elsewhere. Although each such stunt was hailed with newspaper amazement and what-will-they-think-of-next editorials, they were nothing new. *Harper's Weekly* in its issue of February 11, 1871, three full decades before *The Century* was born devoted its front page to this animated scene in which *The Chicago Express*, predecessor of *The Century*, was raced at Poughkeepsie by the ice boats *Zephyr* and *Icicle*. Naturally, the iceboats won. *(Museum of The City of New York.)*

One of the great railroad promotion men of all time, George Henry Daniels *(left)* was by title General Passenger Agent for the New York Central Lines in the nineties and until well after the year 1900. It was he who dreamed up the record breaking run of *The Empire State Express* in 1893 and in the same year *The Exposition Flyer* on a twenty hour run from New York to Chicago. His crowning achievement was *The Twentieth Century Limited* whose every aspect of operation, elegance and distinguished clientele he publicized with such success that riding *The Century* became one of the recognized status symbols in the American scheme of things. Other innovations devised by the fertile Daniels imagination were red capped porters and the parcel checking room. One of Daniels' favorite devices for emphasizing *The Century's* speed and tight schedule were the track pans at frequent intervals along the main line from which, through the agency of a scoop worked by the fireman, water was drawn up into the tender without stopping. They dramatized the urgency which was associated with the train's schedule and the importance of time to its equally important passengers. Here No. 25 takes water from Scotia pans in 1930. *(Above: Rail Photo Service, H. W. Pontin; Left: New York Central.)*

"A School for Courtesy"

Schools for signals, schools to teach the operation of the air brake or for a score of excellent operating purposes have long been conducted by American railroads. But it remained for the

New York Central Lines

to start school attended by ticket sellers, conductors, brakemen, porters, gatemen — to teach courteous responses to the inquiries of the travelling public.

These schools were established because it was deemed good business to have employes equipped with information the travelling public might want and to give it to the public courteously and accurately.

Something of the style and panache of de luxe railroading in 1902 is suggested by the portrait at the top of the page of the first run from its Chicago terminal in June of that year of *The Twentieth Century Limited* over its Lake Shore & Michigan Southern trackage. The high wheeled Prairie type engine, a genuine *rara avis* in fast passenger service, with its polished tires and burnished cylinder heads at the head of four Pullman varnish cars was the apotheosis of elegant travel at the beginning of the century for which the Central's showpiece was named. At the left is a contemporary advertisement of the Central's services. *(Above: Alfred W. Johnson Collection; Below: New York Central.)*

— 21 —

DINNER

HORS D'OEUVRES

Artichoke Hearts in Olive Oil 65   Ripe or Green Olives 25   Midget Gherkins 25   White Onions 25
Chow Chow 25   Sweet Chutney 25   Chilled Celery 45   Sweet Pickled Onions 25

SOUPS

CREAM OF FRESH MUSHROOMS..Cup 25: Tureen 45
CONSOMME, *Hot or Cold* ....Cup 35
OYSTERS *Fried*........................... 85; *Stewed in Milk*................ 65; *Cream*........... 75
CLAM BOUILLON, *Hot or Cold* ....Cup 25
TOMATO JUICE... 30

NEW YORK CENTRAL SPECIAL DINNER

SMALL TENDERLOIN OF BEEF SAUTE
FRESH MUSHROOMS AND GRILLED SPANISH ONION
NEW GREEN PEAS WITH MINT   POTATOES FONDANTE

Choice of

RICE CUSTARD WITH WHIPPED CREAM   APPLE OR MINCE PIE
STEAMED PLUM PUDDING, HARD SAUCE
IMPORTED CHEDDAR CHEESE WITH TOASTED BISCUITS
BREAD AND BUTTER   TEA, COFFEE, MILK

—+—————— [$1.35] ——————+—

SPECIALS TODAY

FRIED FILET OF SOLE, *Tartare Sauce, Julienne Potatoes, Beet and Celery Mayonnaise* 95
BROILED LAKE SUPERIOR WHITEFISH, *Lemon Butter, Escalloped Tomatoes,*
Hashed Browned Potatoes....................... 95
SADDLE OF LAMB *en Casserole, New Peas, Potatoes, Onions and Carrots* 95
FRIED MILK CHICKEN, *Salt Pork, Cream Sauce, New Brussels Sprouts, Mashed Potatoes*....... 95
BAKED SUGAR CURED HAM *Glace, Bigarade, Creamed New Spinach, Sweet Potato Grille*.... 95
SHIRRED EGGS *with Sausage Patties Bordelaise* 65
FRESH VEGETABLES *with Egg* 85
ROAST RIBS OF PRIME BEEF *with Potatoes* 85
ASSORTED COLD MEATS *with Potato Salad* 85
LETTUCE AND TOMATO SALAD, *Russian Dressing*...................................... 40
CANAPE OF GENUINE RUSSIAN CAVIAR 65
SMALL CLUB SIRLOIN *Saute, French Fried Potatoes* 1 25
GRAPE FRUIT, *Iced, Half*... 30
N. Y. C. SPECIAL BAKED APPLE *with Cream*... 30

FROM THE GRILL

Milk Fed Chicken, half, French Fried Potatoes 1 25
Sirloin Steak (for 1), French Fried Potatoes 2 00;   (for 2) 4 00
Rack Lamb Chop (1) 40;   (2) 75   Bacon and Fried Eggs 75   Ham and Fried Eggs 75
Ham 75; Reduced Portion 40   Bacon 75; Reduced Portion 40   Country Sausage 60

FRESH VEGETABLES

MASHED HUBBARD SQUASH.. 30
BOILED ONIONS *in Cream*... 35
NEW BRUSSELS SPROUTS *in Butter*... 40
WHOLE NEW SPINACH *with Egg* 45
CELERY HEARTS, *Demi Glaze*.. 35
NEW CAULIFLOWER *Au Gratin*... 40

Potatoes, Plain Boiled 25   French Fried 35   Mashed 25   Au Gratin 35   Hashed Browned 35
Stewed Tomatoes 30   Small Carrots 30
Royal Mushrooms on Toast 50   Baked Beans, Hot or Cold, with Brown Bread 45

ABOVE PORTIONS PER PERSON ONLY
AN EXTRA CHARGE OF 25 CENTS PER PERSON WILL BE MADE FOR MEALS
SERVED OUT OF DINING CAR

The year 1931 represented by this menu was a depression year and *Century* patrons did themselves well for $1.35, which was less than the $1.50 charged in 1902. In the thirties a *Century* shave was two bits, manicure .75¢ and, after repeal Scotch and soda .60¢. A sleeping car porter averaged $5. in tips per run and his weekly earnings, putting him in the upper brackets of Harlem society, were $38. *(Menu: Courtesy of John Barriger.)*

When *The Century* made its first run back in 1902, the Century Dinner served on this sumptuously appointed diner was $1.50, a price which immediately established the train as a status symbol of the era. Cocktails served in the lounge of the observation car *Eudoxus (left)* were uniformly two bits. *(Two Photos: New York Central.)*

In captioning this full page drawing only a few years before the inaugural run of *The Century*, *Frank Leslie's Illustrated Weekly Newspaper* explained to readers that it depicted no mob scene or civic tumult, but merely the competition for business on the part of hackney carriage proprietors when a prospective fare appeared outside Grand Central Depot. The Grand Union Hotel, facing Grand Central on the south side of Forty-second Street was owned and operated at the time by Simeon Ford, a wit and raconteur of contemporary fame only second to the celebrity of the New York Central's own Chauncey Depew. An anecdote of the time concerned the wag who addressed the Central's President as "Chancey M. Depot, Care The Grand Central Depew." This fairly laid them in the aisles at the Hoffman House and men's bar of the Waldorf Astoria at Fifth Avenue and Thirty-third Street. *(Museum of the City of New York.)*

Chauncey Depew, although no longer President of the New York Central, still drove downtown to its offices daily, piloting his own automobile-car, which was quite a thing in 1902 when most people required chauffeurs, or engineers, as they were then called. (N. Y. HERALD TRIBUNE.)

Forty-second Street at Park Avenue, New York, New York, looking toward the Vanderbilt Avenue corner in 1902, the year *The Twentieth Century Limited* started its run, looked like this. No single automobile marred a vista of carriages and horsecars. In the center background loomed the Manhattan Hotel, then one of the two or three finest in town and birthplace of the Manhattan cocktail. On the southwest corner of Park Avenue where the tall lamp post rises, the Belmont Hotel with its celebrated bar connecting with Grand Central by subterranean passages had yet to appear. Grand Central itself, from which the first *Century* departed on June 15, was still a monument to Victorian taste with its mansard roof, pillared window frames of marble, red brick and retractable striped window awnings. Its quick lunch buffet, predecessor of a later and even more famous oyster bar, was a New York institution, and the transition from one century to another might be symbolized, for those who admired symbolism, by the fact that it was possible to ride up Park Avenue through the discarded tunnel of the old Harlem Railroad on a horsecar to take passage on *The Twentieth Century Limited*, the fastest and finest thing on wheels. *(Museum of The City of New York.)*

On the Lake Shore & Michigan Southern leg of its run *The Twentieth Century Limited* was powered during the first years of its existence by an uncommonly exotic locomotive type, a high wheeled and extremely speedy 2-6-2 or Prairie engine. Even the almost infallible Everett De Golyer, first iconographer of the iron horse in its every American aspect, has been unable to turn up a photograph of *The Century* at speed behind a Prairie, but to suggest the dramatic quality of this portion of its run offers the below photograph of L.S. & M.S. Train No. 85 *The Fast Mail* which followed *The Century* westbound on almost its precise carding with a 2-6-2 on the head end. This he describes as "at the Holy Grail level of scarcity." *(Two Photos: Everett De Golyer Collection.)*

The exotic Prairies, which were reputed to have achieved speeds upwards of ninety miles an hour but had an unfortunate penchant for climbing the rails because of their two wheel leading trucks, were supplanted in 1904 by the celebrated Brooks ten wheelers of the I-1 Class shown on this page. These splendid machines could also live up to the management's expectations that *The Century* go its way like a bat out of hell with the added safety of a four wheel pony truck. In the probably posed photograph above with No. 604 on the point and a five car train, probably in 1904 or 1905, it should be noted that the combination baggage-smoker on the head end bears the inscription "*The Twentieth Century Limited*, New York-Chicago," an indication of the style in which it was even then maintained with specially assigned equipment for its exclusive use. *(Above: New York Central; Below: Everett De Golyer Collection.)*

At the top of the page opposite *The Pennsylvania Limited* is shown in the nineties running backward over the four tracked New York Division through New Jersey behind a 4-4-0 American type engine. This peculiar arrangement obtained westbound as far as Broad Street Station, Philadelphia, which was a stub track terminal, after which it headed for Chicago, as God intended, baggage car first. Mail and baggage *(below)* as well as passengers were loaded at Philadelphia with a minimum of delay. *(Above: Everett De Golyer Collection; Below: John Barriger Collection.)*

The masculine contentments of such fine Pullman-built observation-lounge cars as *Cassius* assigned to *The Pennsylvania Limited* made New York Central management resolve that nothing but the best, also from Pullman, should go into the long awaited *Twentieth Century Limited.* (Pullman Standard.)

Some idea of the lavish appointments of the *Twenty Hour Special*, placed in direct competition to *The Century* in 1902 on the fast new run, may be gained from the three interiors on these pages from the collection of John Barriger. From ornate light globes to fringed and gold embossed valances over the windows they were the finest Pullman could produce. The train itself is shown at the right on its initial run on the historic day of June 15, 1902. *(Pennsylvania Railroad.)*

EUDOXUS

ENDYMION

Among the most beautiful cars built by Pullman for *The Century* in its early years were the compartment-observation-lounge car *Eudoxus* and conventional open section and compartment sleeper *Endymion*, whose exteriors are shown above. At the left, the observation salon of *Eudoxus* testifies to the ample satisfaction of comfort available to the extra-fare traveler in that distant time. (*Three Photos: Pullman Standard.*)

The sketch shown here by the then enormously popular artist Childe Hassam was published in *Harper's Weekly* in 1893 under the title "On The Observation Platform to Chicago." Its obvious inspiration was either the New York Central's twenty hour *Exposition Flyer,* direct forerunner of *The Century,* or The Pennsylvania's competing train on the same run. Whatever its specific setting, it serves to suggest the important role of the brass-railed observation platform in establishing the status of a prestige train both then and for many years to come.

The Century, as was inevitable in its time and on its schedule, figured over the years in numerous accidents of mischance, some of them mere derailments with trifling damage and others catastrophes of a major order. Its worst was a wreck that took place just before daylight on March 29, 1916, at Amherst, Ohio, in which twenty-six persons were killed and forty-five seriously injured. Antecedent to the big pile-up, the first section of the Chicago-Pittsburgh overnight sleeper run eastbound had been stopped by signals at an interlocking tower a mile west of Amherst and, in the deep fog which shrouded the countryside, the second section of the same train crashed into it moments later. The wreckage spilled over onto the westbound tracks and *The Century,* moving at better than sixty miles an hour and behind schedule, piled into the debris before it could be flagged down. *The Century* was derailed by the impact but there were no injuries to either crew or passengers. *(Two Photos: Cleveland Plain Dealer.)*

RED GENERATIONS—There are readers of the Republican in more than twenty towns whose families have been subscribers to this paper for three generations. There must be a reason for it.

PIONEER PAPER OF THE WESTERN RESERVE

THREE TIMES—There are three times as many subscribers to The Republican as there are to any other weekly paper in Lorain County. It is the best and the oldest in Lorain County.

THE ELYRIA REPUBLICAN.

AND WEEKLY TELEGRAM

UNDED JULY 24, 1829. ELYRIA, OHIO, THURS DAY, MARCH 30, 1916. EIGHTY-FOURTH YEAR. NO. 13.

26 ARE DEAD IN WRECK

XTEEN BODIES OUT OF 26 REMOVED FROM N. Y. C. WRECKAGE ARE IDENTIFIED

THE DEAD

Dora Roseberg, 51 Agnes street, ronto, Canada.

Arpad Helgai, Hotel Moreland, veland, President of the Hungar- Theatre Association.

J. H. Hearn, Gallipolis, O.

Frank Gallagher, 40 Heart street, ooklyn.

D. Fruchpman, 92 Girard street, ronto, Canada.

R. Thomas, Fairmont Ave., Phil- elphia.

Mrs. George Prymier, Detroit.

Rev. Gustal Walyi, pastor First Hungarian E. L. church, 53 Thaddeus street, Detroit.

Walter Eason, 1269 Ardin street, Philadelphia.

Rasin Obbah, Indianapolis.

Malzinca Binnoe, 3136 Beach street, Indiana Harbor, Ind.

B. E. Ash, mail clerk, Olmsted Falls.

Charles Nelson, 30, Chicago, machine mover.

Gyorgi Ojonca, Indianapolis, Ind.

INJURED

S. H. Don, 45, Japanese, Haver- Mass., left leg broken and cut ut face.

John Kosnoth, Greek, Home- ed, Pa., broken leg.

Robert Wright, Imperial, Pa., in- red back and head.

Foreign woman, will die.

Louis Lafkovitch, Cleveland, feet t.

F. Bishop, Chicago, fireman.

George Prymier, Detroit.

Two other women injured about body.

R. D. Turner, Clark street, Elyria, fireman, right elbow injured.

H. Gromate, Chicago, marine engineer, badly bruised and cut.

W. A. Manns, Toledo, fireman, burned about face, back sprained.

G. Weseli, Chicago, real estate man, bruised, left for home.

Ollie Osman, badly hurt.

Frank Kellar, Chicago, will die.

Twenty-five persons are dead and nearly a score ounded, some of them fatally, as a result of a rear-end llision between two New York Central passen- r trains, a mile west of Amherst, Wednesday morning ortly after 4:00 o'clock.

To make matters worse the Twentieth Century est bound train crashed into the wreckage 10 minutes er the first and second sections of train 86 had collid- .

The dense fog which prevailed was undoubtedly re- onsible for the wreck, passengers on the first section porting that all efforts to back up the train, failed and e second section crashed through the day coach and ub car.

BROUGHT HERE.

Sixteen victims were rushed to this city on the eepers comprising the first section and were loaded in- ambulances and hurried to Memorial Hospital where ey were lined up in the corridors.

Fourteen of the 25 now known to be dead in the sastrons wreck, have been identified, most of the oth- s being mutilated beyond recognition.

Portions of bodies fairly plastered the engine of e second section of train 86, while arms, legs and ads were dug from the wreckage by the laborers and recking crews engaged in removing what remains of e three trains.

FINE TRAINS

The engineer of the crack Twentieth Century mited, says that when his engine struck the wreck- e of the first section, it was tearing along at 65 miles hour and after being derailed, slid along the rails for ree car lengths, then righted itself and crashed into e second section of the train.

R. D. Turner, of Clark street, fireman on the sec- d section, says the fog was so thick that he could not e 50 feet ahead of the train and the first he knew was hen the engine plowed through the first section.

AWFUL SCENE.

Corpses were strung along the track, wedged on p of the engines and cars and some thrown to the side the right of way.

One man died when the the first section bearing the injured arrived in this city and was taken to the Wilkins-Hurst morgue.

The sight at Memorial Hospital was a heart rending one, stretchers in the corridors being covered with injured persons, while every piece of white cloth in sight bore red stains, some of the nurses appearing as if they had just emerged from a slaughter house.

Every ambulance in th city was at the depot to meet the train bearing the wounded, while the police were called upon to push back the crowd which surged upon the platform.

RENDERED SERVICE

Half a dozen Elyria patrolmen rendered valiant service in recovering bodies from the wreckage, they being among the first to arrive on the scene.

Climbing onto the wrecked engine they removed four mangled corpses from the pilot, the corpse of one woman being found on the top of the boiler.

The Lorain police did not arrive as soon, their auto patrol going into a field near Penfield Junction and narrowly escaping serious injury.

PILES OF CLOTHING.

In the basement of Memorial hospital are twenty piles of blood stained clothing, shoes, hats, etc., some of them have cards pinned on them to show to whom they belong, while others are not marked.

As fast as the doctors were able to operate on the injured they were taken from the emergency ward and placed in rooms on the first second and third floors.

The sun room was turned into an emergency ward, where those slightly injured were given medical attention.

REAL STOICS.

One of the most noticeable things at Memorial hospital, when the injured were awaiting their turn on the operating tables, was the total absence of any outcries from the maimed.

This is typical of foreigners, but while some of them with broken bodies must have been suffering untold pain, they simply closed their eyes, occasionally opening them when someone addressed them.

ENGINEER HANGS ON STEAM PIPE IN TRAIN'S MAD PLUNGE

FLOPS TWICE AND SMASHES AS MANY IN DEATH HAVOC RIDE.

C. C. Robb, of Toledo, engineer on the Twentieth Century limited, relates his harrowing experience, in the two flop and two smashes of the train in which he was in charge.

"We were traveling between sixty and sixty-five miles an hour. I heard the emergency stop whistle, a short shriek, but the fog was so heavy I could not see the head light of my own engine. A second or two after the whistle warning there was a crash. I grabbed the steam pipe. The engine rolled on its side after hitting the first section of No. 86 slid on its side for three car lengths, righted itself, crashed in the second section of train No. 86 and then again turned over on its side. God only knows how I escaped alive."

Robb's hands were burned to a blister in hanging on the steam pipes while the engine continued on its made rampage. Robb had no more than crawled out from the wrecked, miraculously uninjured, when the boiler of the engine he was in charge, exploded.

"I must certainly have a charmed life," said Robb "and I thank God that I can be with my family again."

None of the passengers on the train Robb was engineer of were seriously injured.

PULLED OUT A MAN'S ARM AT THESHOULDER

Fred Roemer, Amherst meat dealer, Carl Ehrman, Amherst grocerman, Frank Mischka, Amherst meat dealer were the first to reach the scene of the wreck of the New York Central at Amherst this morning. They arrived fifteen minutes after the accident. These men with others helped to carry the injured and dying to a special made up train which brought them to Memorial Hospital. Then they assisted in taking care of the dead and to rescue those pinned under the wreckage.

Roemer heard a man beg for help. He was pinned under the wreckage with one arm protruding. Roemer grabbed the man's arm and pulled. A few seconds later the arm severed at the shoulder. "I could help remove the dead and carry the injured and dying but when I looked at the man's arm in my hand it made me sick. It was too much for me," declared Roemer.

NELLIE B. SMITH, SEEKS A DIvorce from her husband, Jasper, on the ground of non-support.

Elyria Man Takes Moving Pictures Of Amherst Wreck

TWO HUNDRED FEET TAKEN FOR PATHE WEEKLY—SHOW IT HERE.

H. M. Marvin, who is preparing to take moving pictures of Elyria the latter part of the week, went to Amherst early this morning and took about two hundred feet of the big New York Central railroad wreck at Amherst. The pictures were taken for the Pathe Weekly and will be shown throughout the country. The pictures will likely be shown in Elyria. The reel was sent to New York this noon.

It is expected that the pictures will be developed and released for New York theatres perhaps on Friday night. The pictures ought to reach Elyria in two weeks at the latest. It will be the quickest action of a large disaster that had not been planned to be given to the motion picture public.

EULOGIZED THE LIFE OF LATE MAX M. SUPPES

Rev. J. H. Grant Paid Splendid Tribute of Respect to the Late Departed.

BEAUTIFUL FLOWERS

SCORES OF PROMINENT MEN FROM VARIOUS SECTIONS OF THE COUNTRY, JOURNEYED TO THIS CITY WEDNESDAY TO ATTEND FUNERAL OF LOYAL FRIEND.

More magnificient floral offerings than those at the Suppes home, on East Bridge street, Wednesday could not be imagined, the living rooms being filled with the most superb display ever witnessed in this city.

Prominent men from all over the United States, journeyed to Elyria, Wednesday, to pay their final tribute of respect to the memory of a dear friend.

Funeral Oration.

The following funeral oration was delivered by Rev. John H. Grant:

The company of Mr. Suppes' friends here gathered is but a small proportion of those who mourn him today. We represent an army of men, not less than 7,000 in number. The steel workers at Lorain under a sense of personal loss. The flag at half-mast is a truthful symbol. The ponderous machineries at rest for an hour are a true sign of sorrowful feeling. One who speaks today should be not only your spokesman but the spokesman of these thousands as well.

Consecrated Man.

Consecration is a word not limited to the field of religion and the church. There are men so unselfishly and tirlessly devoted to the cause of education or civic reform or medical research, that they may justly be named consecrated men

(Continued on page eight.)

GRIM RELIC OF DISASTER

A greusome token of the wreck arrived at the Telegram office in the morning mail in the form of a blood stained post card from Mrs. D. S. Troxel, who is spending the winter at Los Angeles, California.

The card was evidently in one of the mail cars and was picked up by one of the mail clerks and sent to its destination.

LOVED ONES AT HOME WILL WAIT IN VAIN

"Something seems to tell me I won't have you this time next year" is a sentence from an affectionate letter found in a blood stained gray coat whose owner was probably among the dead.

"Well dear I must close it concluded, "I wish I was there to kiss your old bald pate where the brush is the thinnest and count all the dear gray hairs in your head. Bye, bye, darling, I have such a headache I can't see to write any more. Be good daddy. Your own wife—Cora."

MARRIAGE LICENSES.

Carl Christian, 22, Lorain, roll setter, and Hazel Louise Woodinge, 22, Grafton.

NOTICE.

Sons of Veterans special meeting Friday evening, March 31st, reception of members and important business. Lunch will be served.

F. CLAYTON SMITH, Secy.

EARLY ARRIVALS LOOK UPON SICKENING SCENES

Suggest Shambles of War Torn Europe at Amherst Today.

Scenes of horror that beggar description were witnessed by early visitors to scenes of the wreck. A woman's head lay in between the tracks, at one point, hands and feet were scattered about promiscuously. Four stretchers were gathered full of bloody tokens of flesh, bones, limbs pieces of scalp and remnants of unfortunate humans that suggested European battlefields.

A Telegram representative was on the ground before any of the arrivals from Elyria among the first of whom were members of the police force, newspaper men and a stream of sight seekers, followed soon in autos and on the street cars.

County Commissioner Dunn was one of the early arrivals at the scene of the wreck, but when he saw the men gather up three stretcher loads of flesh and bone, he decided he had enough of terrible sights.

One could not step anywhere near the wreck, without seeing a piece of torn and battered flesh on the ground.

Dunn saw a man extricate a woman's head from the wreck, but about all there was left of it unmutilated was a luxuriant mass of hair.

TRAIN NO. 86 FAST CHICAGO-BALTIMORE LIMITED RUN OUTFIT

Train 86 was known as the Pittsburgh-Baltimore-Buffalo Limited, a flyer which made the trip from Chicago to Baltimore in thirteen hours and thirty-five minutes.

It was due in Elyria at 3:09. The train was running a few minutes behind schedule time Wednesday morning.

The train carried sleeping coaches from Chicago to Pittsburgh and Buffalo and took on a sleeper at Cleveland for Buffalo.

It carried a diner from Chicago to Pittsburgh, and was known as one of the finest trains on the New York Central lines.

The flyer was split into two sections Wednesday because of unusually heavy traffic, and this splitting of the train indirectly caused the wreck at Amherst early today.

VICTIMS ARE HORRIBLY MUTILATED

Two Hours Elapsed Before Aid Was Given the Injured.

AIDS IN RESCUE WORK

T. M. WEBB AND W. C. BRADLEY RELATE FRIGHTFUL AGONY OF THOSE INJURED AND DYING FOLLOWING WRECK AND BEFORE ASSISTANCE CAME.—CRASHES TWO MINUTES APART.

It was at least two hours after the wreck that the injured received medical attention, according to T. M. Webb, cf Atlanta, Ga, who was a passenger on the first section of train 86. Webb, with W. Bradley, of Pittsburgh, who was on the second section of train 86, and W. G. Kershaw, of Sommerville, N. J., also a passenger, arrived in Cleveland shortly after 8 o'clock.

"The first section of No. 86 had stopped for a few minutes and was just creeping along when the second section plowed into it," said Webb. "I was lying awake in the Pullman car, third from the end of the first section when the crash came—it was 3:20. The second section must have been going forty miles an hour, I judge, from the impact. The buffet car, which was the last car of the train in our section and the day coach, the second to the last, were hurled onto the west bound track.

"There was an interval of only a few minutes—passengers had not time to realize what actually had happened—when the limited tore into the wreckage.

"Some of those injured in the first crash were killed outright when the limited crashed into the wreckage. I counted at least ten dead and thirty injured and then gave up the task. It was an awful sight—limbs and portions of bodies strewn everywhere.

"It was an hour and twenty minutes before the first physician ar-

(Continued on Page Five).

GENERAL MANAGER MOON TELLS HOW LARGE WRECK HAPPENED

NEW YORK CENTRAL OFFICIAL SAYS SECOND SECTION VIOLATED RULE.

D. C. Moon, general manager of the New York Central Lines, gives this story of the wreck as it was given him from his subordinates on the road at 9 o'clock:

"Here's how the wreck was reported to me:

"Train No. 86, eastbound, was traveling in two sections.

"The engineer of the first section was stopped at Amherst by a signal—I don't know just how.

"The second section of No. 86 should have stopped because of the automatic signal, or by the signal of a flagman on the first section.

"The second section ran into the end coach of the first section. The wreckage from both sections went over on the westbound high-speed track.

"The rear car of the first section was a coach from Chicago to Pittsburg.

"It had forty passengers, four of whom are killed. I don't know how many were injured.

"The next car ahead of the coach was a club Pullman car. There was nobody in this car but a porter and a mail clerk.

"These two men are missing. The cars ahead of the coach and club car were sleepers.

"Nobody in them was hurt.

"The Twentieth Century was derailed, but nobody on it was injured.

"I have ordered an investigation at once.

"I don't think any of the crew was hurt, but so far we haven't got track of the engineer of the second section."

Baby Born On Wrecked Train Shortly After The Accident

PHYSICIANS ON SCENE RENDERED AID.—BOTH WILL SURVIVE.

Mrs. Mary Marston, of Indianapolis, Ind., gave birth to a child in one of the coaches of the second section of train 86 a few minutes after the wreck occurred. Her condition was serious.

Mrs. Marston had expected the visit of the stork in a short time.

Fright, due to the wreck, and the shaking up she was given, caused the birth at this time.

Physicians who were at the scene gave aid to the woman whose child came into the world under such trying circumstances.

EXTRA FARE AND ORCHIDS

If any single tangible aspect of American life in the year 1902 could be said to epitomize the period of splendor in European history and its counterpart in the United States that was known as "La Belle Epoque," it was *The Twentieth Century Limited*. It was the era in Paris of Maxim's on the Rue Royale with its clientele of grand dukes, emperors, champagne salesmen and diamond encrusted ladies of the evening. In London, Edwardian luxury reigned in the stead of Victorian propriety. The wealth of empire converged on the British Isles and was translated into the magnificent living standards of private homes where 200 house footmen in cloth of gold liveries were a commonplace and where the King stylishly ate himself to death in a manner his subjects admired to imitate.

La Belle Epoque in New York was something different but on a comparable scale. Its hallmark at the apex of social eligibility was the Metropolitan Opera where dowagers, weighted beyond handy maneuvering, tottered toward red plush boxes in the Diamond Horseshoe to hear Nellie Melba and Caruso. Equally gilded but less socially exalted were the cabarets and luxury restaurants of Broadway, Rector's, Shanley's, Reisenweber's and roadhouses like Woodmansten where Diamond Jim Brady entertained railroad managers with rare and costly viands he had sent chefs to Europe to discover.

Luxury and ostentation were the predominant elements in *La Belle Epoque* in America and to these was being added something new: speed. Time was discovered to be synonymous with money. A millionaire like Henry C. Frick or Charles M. Schwab's time was too valuable to be needlessly dissipated. Bank cheques and other commercial paper in transit might run up thousands of dollars in interest overnight on the mere passage from Boston or Chicago to New York. Getting from nowhere to nowhere with the utmost available acceleration became and was to remain a preoccupation of people who didn't need to hurry in imitation of people who did. Fast steamers like the *Lusitania* and *Mauretania* were appearing on the Atlantic. Hundred mile an hour speeds for trains had been established as practicable for short distances if not precisely safe, and everywhere that the trains ran, new steel equipment, more powerful engines, heavier rail and better track combined with improvements in train control to step up operating schedules.

La Belle Epoque in the United States was expressed in diamond stomachers, seagoing yachts, liberal waistlines on gentlemen resulting from terrapin for dinner, a dawning appreciation of old masters among millionaires and grand opera at the greatest imaginable expense, all backed and underwritten by gold currency and a dollar as sound as John L. Sullivan's wind.

A fast train, operating on split second scheduling over a long run with luxury equipment available at extra cost to a limited number of patrons was just what 1902 wanted between New York and Chicago.

In accounting for the origins and naming of *The Century* fact and folklore have become, as is their habit, fairly closely entwined, but its age was the dawn of modern publicity in a reasonably responsible dimension as opposed to the P. T. Barnum ballyhoo that had constituted most press agentry until then, and it seems fair to give major credit for *The Century's* evolution to George Henry Daniels. Daniels was the Central's general passenger agent, a short, rotund man with a white goatee, who brought really polished public relations to the Central and who, back in 1891, had dreamed up the truly sensational feat (accomplished two years later) of running *The Empire State Express* with the immortal Charlie Hogan at the throttle of No. 999 at the rate of 112.5 miles an hour. This feat alone, according to Freeman Hubbard, a ranking railroad historian, would entitle Daniels to a place in anybody's hall of fame had he not transcended even this dazzling coup by getting the Postmaster General of the United States to issue a two cent stamp depicting *The Empire State Express* in two colors, thereby creating a collector's item in great demand among philatelists to this very day.

In 1902 Daniels came up with the idea of a train that should run between New York and Chicago, as Stewart Holbrook has it, "like a bat out of hell" and suggested to the moguls of the Central that it be called *The Twentieth Century* as a salute to a new cycle in the Christian time scheme. The *Limited* part came five days afterward to meet the competition of the *Pennsylvania Limited** which was started by the rascally opposition the very same day. Daniels did yeoman service in publicizing *The Century's* every detail of operations including the then vastly spectacular feat of taking water at speed from track pans and kept the city desks alert to the presence of celebrities aboard the flyer that he christened "The Greatest Train in The World." It may well be that he put into the mouth of Bet-a-Million Gates his dual-service remark about who was a suburb of what on the occasion of the maiden run. There were cynics who pointed out that Gates never said anything quotable elsewhere either before or since.

If indeed Daniels inspired Bet-a-Million Gates to *The Century's* first achievement of headlines, and I like to think that he did, there is about his selection a certain significance that bespoke the times themselves. A later event of similar scope

---

*This is the official version of the evolution of the train's name by New York Central archivists. That, in certain circles anyway, it was known from the beginning by the full title it has always run under is suggested by the June 15, 1902 *Chicago Tribune* announcing the train's inaugural run as follows: "The Lake Shore-New York Central's *Twentieth Century Limited* and the Pennsylvania's *Twenty-Hour Special* will make their inaugural trips today, the former leaving here at 12.30 p.m. and the latter at noon."

and magnitude under the auspices of Madison Avenue would not have chosen as its central figure a burly, cigar smoking self-made millionaire in a hard hat and velvet collared paddock coat, wing collar and suit of ratcatcher pattern. It would have draped the pilot of the locomotive with a Hollywood starlet (defined by Gene Fowler as a Los Angeles resident under seventy not explicitly engaged in prostitution) in diaphanous attire and the meaningless smirk of vacuous femininity with a ribband draped across her middle engrossed with the legend "Miss New York-Chicago." In comparison, Gates seems an altogether admirable choice.

It would be possible, of course, to take the emergence, rise, flowering and decline of *The Twentieth Century Limited* as a microcosm of American style and taste in the period of its lifetime. Hotels, ocean liners and crack trains are uncommonly accurate benchmarks for the charting of social and economic geology, and if the decline of railroad travel in favor of the infamies and inconveniences of air travel may be taken as an index of American living, the graph is a melancholy one indeed. The present enquiry is, however, solely concerned with the character and operation of The Greatest Train in The World, and its social and economic implications may be left to more austere and, of necessity, less cheerful evaluation.

Until three years before the inaugural run of *The Century*, Pullman had been what amounted to a dirty word wherever the writ of Vanderbilt ran. Back in the time of the old Commodore, the New York Central and its affiliates had started doing business with George Mortimer Pullman's great and hated rival, carbuilder Webster Wagner, whose Wagner Palace Carbuilding Company had from that time on supplied all sleepers, diners, parlor cars and special equipment, including scores of eye-popping private cars, for the New York Central & Hudson River Railroad, the Boston & Albany, the Lake Shore & Michigan Southern and other Vanderbilt lines. The arrangement had been eminently satisfactory to both contracting parties. The Wagner cars were magnificently built and designed, their service and staffing faultless and their resources of luxury and safety so closely approximating those of their Pullman opposite numbers that Pullman at length claimed more than coincidence was involved and brought a million dollar suit in Federal court for patent infringements.

Like Pullman, Wagner not only built its own cars, but operated them under franchise over the Vanderbilt lines, and its hand picked staffs of porters, barbers, lady's maids, chefs, waiters and club car attendants were headed by Wagner conductors whose distinctive uniforms included a winter greatcoat with an attached cloak lined with red satin. Wagner had great class, and it was proven socially when the President of the Wagner Company, Dr. William Seward Webb, married Eliza Osgood Vanderbilt, granddaughter of the Commodore, thus cementing the Wagner and New York Central interests in what Mr. Dooley called gilt edge bonds of matrimony. Shortly thereafter, Dr. Webb also became President of the Lake Shore & Michigan Southern, which reaffirmed the advantages of being a Vanderbilt in-law.

The romance between Wagner and the Vanderbilt lines had been a durable one over the years, unmarred by the melancholy circumstances that the founder of the carbuilding firm, Webster Wagner, had been killed in a wreck at Spuyten Duyvil while riding one of his own cars in a New York Central train.

In 1899, however, Pullman at length prevailed as it had over all the rest of the competition, and the Wagner Company was absorbed into Pullman and shortly disappeared from the general awareness. The last cars Wagner built as an independent firm were a series of uncommonly fine sleepers and diners for the *Lake Shore Limited*, immediate predecessor of *The Twentieth Century Limited* as flagship of the New York Central fleet of passenger trains.

The first important order on Pullman's books from the Central was for equipment for the newly projected *Century*. The railroad took a long look at the competition in the form of the Pennsylvania whose *Pennsylvania Limited*, opposite number of *The Lake Shore Limited* on the Chicago run, was being hailed as "the most beautiful train in the world", at least as of that moment. Pullman had outdone itself on the *Pennsylvania Limited*. Its famed Marquetry Room had gone into a trance and produced ecstacies of inlaid satinwood, rosewood and primavera. Passengers nested amidst thickets of potted palms and stalked their before-dinner Manhattans, for it was the heyday of the whiskey cocktail, in jungles of hassocks, overstuffed chaise lounges and growing shrubbery. The Pennsylvania was an operation of great style and distinction and the Central used it as a yardstick. "Give us something finer than the Pennsy," it said in effect to Pullman.

In the matter of exterior decor affecting both its cars and locomotives, the New York Central and the allied Vanderbilt roads were heir to an overall austerity, a sort of mortmain that had been in effect and dated from the days of The Commodore himself. In the Central's formative years when the elder Vanderbilt had been busy merging the various component carriers that were to become the New York Central & Hudson River Railroad, there had been no inhibition against bright colors for rolling stock and an abundance of stunning gold trim, brass, red finelining and other fanciful elegance about engines. The Commodore's own private car was a stunner with scenes painted all over its sidewalls and bulkheads depicting Niagara Falls and other points of interest along the railroad right of way. It was good advertising and the Commodore was nobody to let his light shine under any bushel. His private engine was splendid with mahogany cab, gold trim and a magnificent storm lantern for a headlight, with the Commodore's likeness, whiskers, stock collar and countenance of benevolent rapacity all depicted in the side panels. The regular passenger equipment was only slightly less delightful.

During one of the old gentleman's recurrent donnybrooks with the stockholders, however, some churl circulated the rumor that the brass trim and engine bell on the President's private locomotive were fashioned from purest gold with the implicit suggestion that it represented just so much money out of the stockholders' pockets. The same curmudgeon implied that the circus-wagon decor of the Vanderbilt private car did no good to the dignity of the road and merely served to gratify a vulgar penchant for ostentation.

In a towering rage at this canard, the Commodore banished everything that could be construed as superfluous ornamentation from the Central's equipment and its subsidiaries. Gone was the gold trim on engines and the glorious spread eagles from their tenders. Gone with the wind were the splendid yellow coaches and varnished mahogany parlor cars. From being a railroad of outward and visible magnificence, the Central emerged in strictly utilitarian attire, for all the world like the black bombazine of Hetty Green. In 1902 the Commodore's ruling still obtained and the exterior of *The Twentieth Century Limited* was ordained in standard Pullman green and it was to be drawn by motive power whose austerity was almost painful.

Although Wagner, so long the favored court car-builder to the Vanderbilt lines, had been absorbed by Pullman three years before the inaugural of *The Century*, much of the early *Century* equipment was Wagner hand-me-down composite and observation cars which, according to Arthur D. Dubin, doyen of authorities on old time passenger equipment, had been originally outshopped for *The Lake Shore Limited*. The sleeping cars were authentic Pullmans, also from *The Lake Shore* pool re-stenciled with *The Century* insigne and it was not until 1903-04 that they were replaced by Pullmans especially and explicitly designed for *Century* service.

Whether a barber was included in the personnel of the first *Century* is not apparent from the record, but he came into his well publicized own in 1904 with the arrival from Pullman of the buffet-library-smoking car *Indiana* containing a smoking room with overstuffed furniture, two sections for the accommodation of bridge whist and poker, a library "with the best class of periodicals and a completely appointed barber shop and bathroom."

When the first all-steel Pullmans arrived to be incorporated in *The Century* in 1910, they included buffet No. 449 whose exterior sidewalls were grooved steel to simulate wooden construction in order to allay the fears of passengers who imagined that electrocution might be a byproduct of riding steel cars in thunderstorms. It was an innocent deceit widely practiced not only by the Central but other contemporary railroads including the New Haven. The barber on this splendid conveyance not only trimmed beards for the modest sum of two bits but provided "refreshing baths with sea salt if desired."

Over the years *The Century* barbers became an integral part of the folklore of the train itself. They shaved, trimmed and singed the mighty and were rewarded with fat fees and tips on the stock market

which allowed several of them to retire in well upholstered ease. A notable tonsor was named Al Romano who held court aboard the club-lounge car *Van Twiller* in the early thirties. Al Smith made him a gift of a fine pocket watch and his special clip for clerics attracted favorable attention of Cardinal Spellman and he regularly visited St. Patrick's Cathedral on the New York end of the run to trim the archiepiscopal locks.

The legendary smoothness of *The Century's* passage over the Water Level Route encouraged shaves among even the most timid who normally viewed a straight razor at eighty miles an hour with distrust. The Central had to caution several barbers against making cracks about the chances of getting one's throat cut on the not-so-smooth run of the opposition *Broadway Limited*.

A publicity release from the New York Central's promotion department described the equipment of the first run as follows:

"The trains will be composed of buffet, smoking and library, composite cars *Decius, Cyrus,* observation cars *Alroy* and *Sappho,* 12 section drawing-room state-room cars *Petruchio, Philario, Gonzalo* and *Benvolio.* These trains express the latest art in carbuilding. No effort or expense has been spared to provide the traveling public with all the comforts and conveniences that are afforded by the highest grade hotels, the furnishings and fittings being complete in every detail. The exterior of the car is painted Pullman standard color, the ornamentation in gold being simple, but very artistic; gothic lights and oval windows of stained glass set in metal frames lend additional beauty to the exterior elevation. The interior finish is of specially selected hard woods, embellished with delicate marquetry; the seat coverings, carpets, ceilings, etc., being of self toned colors which harmonize with the woods used. A particularly noticeable feature is the absence of all heavy carvings, ornate grilles and metal work, stuffy hangings, etc.; the simplicity and quiet elegance of design, combined with the beauty of the natural wood, being relied upon entirely for decorative effect.

"The trains are illuminated throughout by electricity — generated by the axle system — and ventilated by electric fans. Each center lamp has four 16 C. P. incandescent lamps. In the sleeping cars each section is provided with a reading lamp, which enables patrons to read, after retiring, if they so desire. In the smoking and observation rooms, side reading lamps are placed in convenient locations, and side lamps are also placed over each table in the dining cars. Ladies will especially appreciate the commodious dressing rooms, furnished with dresser, seats, electric curling-iron heater and hot and cold water and many other conveniences.

"A general but brief description of each car is as follows:

"The buffet library smoking car contains a spacious smoking room seating thirty persons, equipped with luxurious easy chairs, two sections being provided for those who desire to play cards; a library equipped with standard literature and all of the best class of periodicals, a completely appointed barber shop and bath room, a writing desk with suitable stationery, and a buffet from which light refreshments, wines, etc., are served.

"The dining car has five double tables, seating four persons each, and five single tables, seating two each. These cars are very attractive, being finished in choice Santiago mahogany. All the equipment, linen, silverware, crockery, etc., were manufactured to order.

"The sleeping cars contain twelve sections and a drawing room and a stateroom, the rooms being connected by folding doors, so that they may be used separately or *en suite*. Ample toilet facilities are provided for both men and women. These cars are finished in vermillion wood and marquetry.

"The observation car has six compartments, finished in mahogany, Circassian walnut, satinwood and primavera. The large observation room is finished in vermillion wood and equipped with comfortable chairs and sofas and a writing desk. A large observation platform affords an exceptional opportunity for viewing the scenery en route."

Considering the epochal nature of the event, the first runs of *The Century* were without incident, and Bet-a-Million Gates' remark was the only tie-in with the glamor world that has survived.

By comparison, the maiden voyage of the Pennsylvania's competing flyer which seems from contemporary accounts to have started life as *The Twenty Hour Special* was positively fraught with excitements. "The train which started from Chicago with every berth excepting five uppers full had many obstacles to overcome," reported *The Chicago Tribune*. "Nothing but the greatest determination pulled the crew through."

On this Horatio Alger note the account went on to detail how, just west of Alliance, Ohio, "No. 30 encountered a runaway freight train. The passenger crew soon had it under control and got behind it and pushed it two miles to the nearest siding, switched it in and continued on its way."

After this contretemps another freight train on the main line delayed its clearing Alliance which put the flyer twenty minutes off the advertised schedule. All but two minutes of this was, however, recovered by Pittsburgh which it left five minutes off because, when the sleeper *Bryn Mawr* from St. Louis was cut into the consist, "the air man had made a defective connection and the train had to slow up after running a hundred yards."

In order to get back on schedule, the engineer who is identified as "Big Cal Miller" ran the four miles between Cove and Duncannon along the Susquehanna River at a rate of ninety-five and four tenths miles an hour, a carding which must have given the passengers their money's worth of thrills if they were awake at the time. The Pennsylvania train was a far heavier consist than the original *Century* and included three conventional Pullman sleepers, presumably with open sections and drawing rooms, an observation-sleeper-drawing room car, parlor car, diner and baggage-mail car.

It may be of interest to students of railroad history that the inaugural runs of The Pennsylvania's *Twenty-Hour Special* and *The Twentieth Century Limited* spurred competition among the lesser carriers for a share of the high speed traffic between Chicago and the East. On June 15, 1902 in its account of the first runs of the Pennsylvania and Central flyers, *The Chicago Tribune* remarked: "The Michigan Central has also arranged to put on, commencing today, a limited train between Chicago and New York that will make the time in twenty-four hours. An extra charge of $4. will be made on this train. The Erie is also talking of putting on a twenty-four hour train between Chicago and New York, and, if it does, the Wabash is almost certain to do the same thing."

As long as *The Century* remained a luxury train and the pride of a proudly administered railroad, direct competition to its prestige, equipment and schedule was maintained by the Pennsylvania Railroad's *Broadway Limited*, also a meticulously operated flyer for which its management made almost identical claims with those the Central made for *The Century*. Over the years, *The Broadway's* timecard was adjusted up or down to keep exact pace with *The Century* schedule. If one train added an innovation of luxury, its opposite number followed suit with the speed of light. In 1938, *The Broadway* was streamlined by Raymond Loewy, and Central executives were a bundle of nerves until Henry Dreyfuss could do the same thing for *The Century*. Both trains were all-Pullman, extra fare, super de luxe as long as the competition between them lasted. Their progress was an elegance sweepstakes that claimed national attention and partisanship.

The year 1938 was epochal beyond the confines of the New York Central for it was then, when *The Century* appeared in its new exterior livery of battleship gray with white trim, that the long familiar dark green of Pullman Standard began disappearing from the carriers everywhere in favor of regionally favored liveries of brighter colors as well as the severe steel sheen of shotwelded manufacture.

Curiously, neither *The Century's* character nor that of the rival *Broadway* derived in predominant measure from the New York that was their common terminal. No carrier in the record seemed ever to be an extension of New York's personality. The trains of the New Haven were more closely related in their character to Boston than to Manhattan. The Baltimore & Ohio, although its crack runs for many decades terminated at the Hudson, was more of a Southern carrier than anything else. The Reading, of course, was pure Philadelphia in its every overtone. The Erie assumed the coloring of the Southern Tier. *The Broadway Limited* owed its allegiance to Philadelphia and the Main Line patronage of its suburbs, and its sailing lists were fragrant with Biddles, Cassatts, Wideners and Cadwaladers, Strawbridges and Stotesburys. Often a ponderable proportion of its passengers boarded or left the Pullmans at Paoli after that aristocratic faubourg was established as an operational stop in the Pennsy electrification.

The Century was a Chicago train, first, last and always, and to that degree justified Bet-a-Million Gates' prophecy that it would make New York a suburb of Lake Michigan.

As long as the two trains were maintained on terms of comparable equality, *The Century* and *The Broadway* each had its active partisans and even enjoyed the loyalty of entire families from one generation to the next like Harvard and Yale, White Star and Cunard and patronage of The Plaza or St. Regis Hotels in New York. "He'll be on *The Century*," or "You'll catch him on *The Broadway*" could be said of hundreds of regular travelers whose devotion to one train or the other was a well established facet of their personalities. Business associates who saw eye to eye in other matters of greater importance had a last drink together at the bar of the old Manhattan Hotel and would meet again next day at the Blackstone in Chicago, but at 5:30 they snapped their watches shut and their ways diverged toward Grand Central and Penn Station. In the night they would ride parallel through the dark hours, as remote from one another as planets on their courses and as infallible in their conjunctions.

Out of their New York terminals, the *Century* and *Broadway*, although they might depart at the same minute, diverged in almost diametrically opposite directions up the Hudson and through New Jersey, respectively, and never passed within viewing distance of each other throughout the night. As the two mainlines converged on Chicago, however, they ran for some miles side by side around the southern end of Lake Michigan and, if the trains were on exact schedule, they were visible to each other running westward in the morning or east in the late afternoon through a vista of industrial installations, telegraph poles and bridge structures.

When *The Broadway* and *The Century* ran parallel to each other, their engines looking like a photo finish at Latonia, passengers in each of the flyers would crowd to the window to watch the competition and make subdued cheering sounds if their cars finally drew ahead. The engineers were not permitted to race and the trains' acceleration as they left Englewood was often conditioned by the tonnage of the day and motive power involved, but it always looked like a race and the passengers loved it.

Now and then disaster overtook *The Century* as mischance will occur in all human undertakings. The wreck in which *The Century* participated without injury to any of its own passengers or crew at Amherst, Ohio, is described in a picture spread in this book.

A far more melancholy wreck took place at Mentor, Ohio, twenty-two miles east of Cleveland on the night of June 21, 1905, involving No. 25 on the westbound run and resulting in the death of fourteen passengers and five crew members including the engineer. It became a classic in the category of catastrophes attributable to an open switch. It also attracted uncommon attention, much of it far from favorable, because it happened only four days after the original twenty-hour schedule had been shortened to eighteen hours and many railroaders of the time entertained grave doubts about the prudence and practicability of such a tight operation.

Engineer Tyler and Fireman Gorham were calling signals regularly as the train bore down on the sleeping village of Mentor at about sixty miles an hour. Both men confirmed to each other that the facing point switch into the station siding showed white, indicating that it was properly lined, but when the pilot was no more than 300 feet away, Tyler shouted, in the immortal phrase of Casey Jones, "Jump, Gorham! Jump!" The fireman realized that to unload at that speed was sure destruction and, not knowing what had alarmed the engineer, crouched behind the backhead of the boiler just as the engine hit the open switch and, at unabated speed, turned into the house track.

A chaotic pileup ensued instantly as the train left the track and crashed into the station building. The engine described a complete somersault and landed upright facing the direction from which it had come. The first car, traditionally a combine with baggage and a buffet section, caught fire immediately and the fatalities listed above resulted.

Investigation disclosed that the switch was improperly aligned and its lamp extinguished. It had been inspected, according to his story, by the station agent only a few minutes before in accordance with regulations governing the approach of Trains 25 and 26, and he swore at the enquiry that it was in proper order when he returned to his post. Nobody else had been seen in the vicinity and it was supposed, but never proven, that the agent had mistakenly opened the points in a moment of panic. Numerous similar cases are on record in which an employee charged with lining a switch has, at the last moment as a train approached, thrown it open apparently under the hysterical impression that he had not properly done his duty. The opening of switches by otherwise entirely blameless employees in the path of speeding trains became so common that regulations on many carriers required brakemen charged with lining the track to stand on the side of the track across from the switch stand after he had performed his work.

The Mentor wreck greatly disturbed the Central and provided a field day for the Cassandras who felt that an eighteen hour schedule between New York and Chicago was plainly against God and an invitation to disaster.

To trace the scheduled operations of *The Twentieth Century Limited* in its constantly changing variations of carding, consist and equipment, its mutations of departure and arrival hours, the ebb and flow of traffic in accordance with the economic times, would be largely a thankless task and not the office of a biographer more concerned for the style and character of the train over the decades than for the minutiae of either its appointments or dispatchings. The personality of *The Century* for more than fifty years was a constant; only its details were variables.

Let us select, however, as a paradigm, a representative year and examine in some detail the profile, appearance and conduct of *The Century* in, say, 1929, before the stock market cataclysm cast a shadow over the national economy and before the looming 1941 war inflated it unduly.

In 1929 the regularly assigned *Century* was supplemented in both directions by an equally stylish train with identical luxury equipment known as *The Advance Twentieth Century Limited* which left Grand Central at 1:45 in the afternoon, an hour before the then sailing time of the conventional section and running on the same schedule to arrive in Chicago an hour earlier on a twenty-hour carding. Out of Chicago the eastbound *Advance Century* was scheduled to leave at 11:40 with 12:40 the advertised departure of the parent train. *The Advance Twentieth Century Limited*, which was a few years later to be supplanted by the *Commodore Vanderbilt*, was also extra fare and in every detail of management and operations indistinguishable from the main sections save one: both eastbound and westbound it served luncheon to almost everybody on board. So did the eastbound *Century* leaving Chicago at 12:40, while luncheon was available, but not heavily patronized on the westbound train out of New York at 2:45 p.m.

In these times of teem and prosperity *The Century* was not the all-room train it was to become within the next decade. It offered open section uppers and lowers as well as drawing rooms, staterooms and compartments, and the service charge or extra fare was a flat $9.60 per passenger over and above the standard rail fare of the time and whatever Pullman space the patron might elect. A few years later when the author of this monograph started riding *The Century* as a regular, the fare was a flat $50, including surcharge each way and it cost an even hundred dollar bill to get to Chicago and back or vice versa. Although upper berths were available, the demand for them was in decline as travel became more and more sophisticated and a request to the ticket clerk for "a berth" had come to imply a lower unless an upper, as alternate, was specifically named. The way was being paved for the all-room car train although the roomette was not yet on Pullman's drawing board.

No train in the world was more flexible than *The Century* or more available to enlargement and expansion as its space might be in request. There were years on end when two and three sections in each direction were the rule rather than the exception and at times of political conventions, football games or other events of importance at its terminals, six and seven sections were handled with almost equal aplomb. *The Century* was a money making train. The New York Central was in business in those days to make money. The management was agreeable to as many trains as the traffic warranted and assembled them as dexterously as a competent domestic staff might accommodate an extra guest for dinner. Only close scrutiny reveals the enormous complexity of such an operation.

Supposing that through some concatenation of important events in the East or Middle West, there were seven sections of the regular train running in a single direction against the conventional two or three in the opposing run as well as *The Advance Twentieth Century Limited* and whatever might be required for the Boston section, there might well be close to a dozen versions of *The Century* between terminal and terminal on a given night, each with an average consist of a postal car, club car, eight sleepers, one diner and one observation-club-sleeping car. Taking into consideration that only specially selected Pullman equipment with decor and furnishings acceptable to the management were starred on the Pullman list as being available to assignment in Trains No. 25 and 26, it will be apparent that an enormous pool of passenger cars must be available in the coach yards of Mott Haven and its opposite number, Root Street yard in Chicago.

Christmas and Thanksgiving were the only days in the year when the Central's traffic department could be sure of running *The Century* in a single train in each direction uncomplicated by last minute demands for problematic amounts of sleeping space. There never was an extra section on either of these characteristically domestic holidays.

Staffing a train of such unpredictable dimensions was a problem shared of course by the Pullman Company and the Central jointly since Pullman owned cars were operated by Pullman directed staffs of Pullman conductors, porters, barbers, club car attendants and special service functionaries. The train crews charged with the operation of the train movement, conductors, brakemen, enginemen and firemen on the engine and baggagemen in the baggage compartment of the club car were the responsibility of the operating railroad. The dining car crews were also New York Central employees. This pattern was occasionally complicated by the inclusion of a club car under Pullman management and another at the other end of the train owned by New York Central and having one of its employees as the club car attendant. The permutations were limitless and are recommended to advanced students with a taste for mathematics.

Give thought to the problem presented by the necessity for recruiting six extra train barbers on two hours' notice, each personable and acceptable to the quality clientele of a de luxe train and each professionally adept at shaving a customer at seventy miles an hour without cutting his throat. Or pause to consider the requisitioning of the appropriate number of racks of spring lamb, Virginia hams and minute breakfast steaks for six extra dining cars with an eye to the season, which often determines meat consumption, and the sneaky appearance on the calendar of Friday and other religious fast days of several faiths. Liquor, cigarettes, cigars, playing cards and most of items carried in stock on the club car were fairly durable, but the perishables involved in restaurant management, cut flowers and free newspapers can run into a tidy sum one way or the other.

A good average day in 1929 would see twenty-five cars filled with sleeper space purchasers out of New York with four carloads more to be added at Albany from the Boston section. This, together with the proper complement of club cars, diners and observation lounge cars was sufficient to account for three sections westbound of *The Twentieth Century Limited*. If three trains were being handled, the mail usually rode Third 25 in a single car, two at the most. The third section stopped at all large cities across the State of New York for both mail and passengers, the advance sections making only routine and operational stops at Harmon, Albany, Syracuse, Buffalo, Cleveland, Toledo and Elkhart. The postal cars carried letter mail and daily papers only. Pouches of mail in excess of the capacity of the sixty-foot Railway Post Office cars on this run were carried in the baggage compartment of the adjoining club car and transferred to the R.P.O. car for sorting. Sorted or "worked" mail would be then moved back to baggage compartment if additional space was required in the R.P.O. car for the working of mail. No mail storage cars were ever hauled on *The Century*. The Boston section over the rails of the Boston & Albany east and west from the Hudson River to Massachusetts Bay was less aloof. Two and three mail storage cars, as well as the single sixty-foot R.P.O. car, often rode on the drawbar of the B. & A.'s square domed Hudsons and not infrequently an iced reefer of fresh whitefish from Lake Michigan or Boston scrod and oysters for the west went ahead of the Pullmans. These originated or were cut out at Albany in an operation that eventually lost so much time from *The Century's* carding that the Boston section was eliminated in favor of *The New England States*, Nos. 27 and 28.

Although it might appear from the heterogeneous duties assigned to it that the last section was the least favored of the several *Centuries*, the fact was quite the opposite. Although it worked

mail and passengers along the route, it was the one train that ran precisely on the carded schedule and arrived at its terminal on the dot of time. Other sections ran ahead of it and had to accommodate themselves to its meticulous progress according to the timecard.

The rolling stock that went into the pool devoted to servicing *The Century* in the twenties and thirties was made up of Pullman sleeping equipment maintained and operated by Pullman and a sprinkling of Pullman operated club cars or buffets. An experienced traveler could tell which ownership of car he was on because the railroad made its own cocktails to the individual order of each customer, Pullman barmen used bottled Martinis, Manhattans and Old Fashioneds most of them by Heublein. This, of course, before prohibition and after repeal.

The classical car names attributed by legend to the selection of George M. Pullman's daughter, Florence, later Mrs. Frank O. Lowden, and the random place names to accord with runs assigned to specific cars plus a handful named for living celebrities—Amon Carter of Forth Worth often occupied the drawing room of the Pullman sleeper *Amon G. Carter* on the Pennsylvania's *Spirit of St. Louis*, to St. Louis as did Adolphus Busch, another favored patron of the train—had mostly disappeared in favor of a less ornate and imaginative classification by prefixes which baffled yardmasters less and assisted things generally all down the line.

Entire generations of yardmasters, trainmasters and even the porters assigned to them had found difficulty with *Heraclites*, *Acanthus*, *Agamemnon* and *Herodotus*, but *Glen Ayrie*, *Night Sky* and *American Marine* gave them less trouble and it no longer required a combination classical scholar and chambermaid to make down lower six. It also gave fewer bad moments to telegraph operators reporting the train consist and availability of space.

The *Glen* cars assigned to *The Century*, *Glen Lomond*, *Glen Ayrie*, *Glen Nevis* were all-stateroom cars with six compartments and three drawing rooms and on the New York Central ran only in *The Century* and its counterpart on the St. Louis haul, *The Southwestern Limited*. Some confusion prevailed at one time because the management wanted only *Glens* with walnut finish for *The Century*, leaving mahogany for the St. Louis customers, but this was a minor matter. The last four-teen open-section sleepers on *The Century* were the *Star* series: *Starlight*, *Starbright*, *Starfish*, *Starucca*; the twelve-section-and-drawing room sleepers were *Easts*: *East Rochester*, *East Albany*, *East Grove*, etc. The record fails to show if there was *East Lynne*.

The *Central* category comprised observation lounge cars and was restricted to *The Century* while Pullman standard sleepers were in a similar but easily distinguishable class with a *Central* prefix: *Centralia*, *Centurion* and *Centalpina*. There was also a *Valley* classification at the time of which we write, *Maumee Valley*, *Mohawk Valley* and the like, uncommonly handsome observation lounge cars with sleeping accommodations on a limited scale comprising drawing rooms *en suite* with single bedrooms. The master stateroom suite with shower was not to appear until the all-room *Century* a full decade in the future.

In times of crisis, usually occasioned by the Great Lakes weather but sometimes generated by human or structural failure, the entire collective will power of the New York Central System seemed to focus on getting *The Century* through with the least possible delay. High priority freight might freeze to the tracks at Buffalo and other ranking trains go into the hole all the way from Cleveland to Elkhart, but extra gangs and flangers, wedge plows and helper engines diverted from other runs combined to get the line's crack varnish over the road with the least possible damage to its schedule and operational pride. Harry Lee Stewart, a long time *Century* admirer and patron who first knew it in the years before 1910 and lived to ride it in streamlined Diesel, recalled being aboard one night soon after the 1941 war when snow lay in inches and drifted in feet everywhere west of Syracuse. "At midnight," he recalled, "already late we passed the westbound *Commodore Vanderbilt* pulled by a double-header of J-3a's completely stalled in the far right track amidst high drifts. It was then I learned we were progressing directly behind a snowplow and that we had a mighty Niagara coupled ahead of the road Diesel, all pulling furiously . . . We were but a few hours late into Chicago."

The Century gave the passengers extra service for their extra fare.

For many years the New York Central's main-line, improbably enough, ran through town right down the main street of Syracuse in upper New York. The westbound train was scheduled to go through in the middle of the evening about the time dinner was being served and patrons of the diner and club car could and did raise glasses to the equally affable patrons of the town's saloons visible through the windows and engaged in mutually satisfactory occupations at their respective oases. Now and then a Syracusan more than ordinarily in wine would attempt to climb aboard the observation platform as the train progressed at snail's pace down the thoroughfare and a brakeman was stationed there against this contingency. Part of the charm of the trip vanished when the Central's tracks were rerouted around the town.

Both east and west sections of *The Century* afforded well publicized views of the Hudson Valley save during the shortest days of the year, and in midsummer it was daylight all the way to and from Albany, and beyond Albany into the Mohawk Valley. At the Chicago end of the run, however, some of the most rewarding scenes of lovely prairies and rolling farmlands west of Elkhart were seldom seen by the commonality of passengers who slept through them westbound and passed them in the dark at most seasons eastbound. The occasional early bird who sought the observation car half an hour out of Elkhart had scant company save drowsy members of the train crew, but he saw an uncommonly appealing part of the American landscape for his trouble.

Over its curves and spirals *The Century* rolled in soundless tranquility, past sagging wooden depots and baggage rooms that had been venerable when Dewey took Manila, while switch engines took to sidings in deference to the imperial passage and crossing tenders retired to their shanties as the rear markers flashed by. Milk trains and occasional locals with two coaches behind a wheezing ten wheeler were overtaken and passed like mendicants peering from the roadside at the progress of a proconsul. It was a world of country things and amiable obsolescences and, for the moment of its going, it all belonged to *The Century*.

By and large, however, and over the years, the clientele of *The Century* was not the sort to take much interest either in scenery or, with rare professional exceptions, the operations of a railroad. Their preoccupations were with big business and weighty affairs and more familiar with Dow's bulletins than with Thoreau or Thomson's "Seasons".

Less dramatic, always, than its departure and savoring somehow of anticlimax was the arrival at its twin terminals of *The Century* or its several sections as the case might be. Chicago was a citadel of gloom for full six months of the year and the ice encrusted platforms of the long train bays at La Salle were sanded with rock salt and swept by gelid winds from Lake Michigan that made egress from the warm cars a depressing experience. The subcellar from which taxis were dispatched was an abode of profane language and badly lit chaos at *Century* time, and experienced travelers went directly down the depot steps and through the lobby to a usually more expeditious rendezvous with Jehu in La Salle Street itself.

Arrival in New York, because it was underground, avoided elemental gloom but was still somehow characterized by a certain stealth and furtiveness always associated with our caveman inheritance. Debarking passengers in the grip of mild hangovers acquired in the club car and the dishevelment peculiar to making one's toilet on trainboard, no matter what the advertising and promotion said, forged through the traingate wondering if they had a guilty look to the hard faced characters who scanned their emergence and were supposed, by popular legend, to be plain clothes detectives looking for wanted persons.

The Century's arrival each morning was announced over the loud-speaker in Station U. at Fifty-seventh Street under Park Avenue to the copy operator sitting at his desk in Tower A above the incoming platforms. "Train 26 by N. K. at 9:20 a.m." The copy operator repeated the message to the director seated beside him: "Train 26 by N. K. at 9:20 a.m." Seven telephones, a loud speaker, signal boards and a track map covered with moving lights surrounded the director. Choosing their route, he called to the four levermen standing at their console: "2 to 1 to 40." "2 to 1 to 40" echoed the levermen like a Gilbert & Sullivan chorus, throwing appropriate handles. Wheels whirred; gears clanged. On the tracks switches aligned themselves and signals changed from red to yellow. Simultaneously the message was received at ten

bulletin boards located throughout the station. In the Vanderbilt Avenue waiting room its import appeared on the west wall bulletin board. In their dressing room twenty-seven redcaps in front of twenty-seven full length mirrors put final touches on their uniforms and pushed caps to a jaunty angle. Chief of Red Caps, Jim Williams, hurried from wherever he was at the moment to be on hand and baggage handlers and mail men manned their electric trucks to be near the head end revenue car when it stopped.

At 9:30 *The Century* came to rest with a sigh of releasing air and the simultaneous thunder of sixteen metal Pullman doors banging open.

Passengers of special importance were met by Chief Red Cap Williams, or, on state occasions, by Miles Bronson, the terminal manager. Franklin D. Roosevelt once gave Williams an autographed photo instead of a tip. Alfred E. Smith once gave him a brown derby hat. Gene Fowler, more practical, gave him $5.00 for retrieving a portable typewriter he had left way back yonder in the club car. Fowler was at the time in the high brackets at Hollywood and received compensation in the form of $1,000 cash at the end of each day at the studio. He felt the industry might not last until Saturday. On the morning of the misplaced typewriter he had encountered Richard Berlin, chief of the Hearst magazines, in the observation car after dinner and was subject to the shakes.

After the passengers had all gone their ways the porters turned in whatever articles of property they had contrived to leave behind them to Lost & Found. The three items most frequently forgotten by *Century* patrons were false teeth, pyjama tops and jewelry.

An infinite variety of painstaking detail went into the ordering of *The Century's* affairs and appearance which might individually be lost to the casual beholder but which in their sum added up to making it a strictly de luxe operation.

On arrival at the New York end of the run, for example, the train, once the passengers were ashore, must be returned to Mott Haven yards in several sections for realigning on the service tracks against the return trip. Observation cars and club cars must be turned, for their construction was such that they cannot be run in both directions. So must diners, for, whatever might be the practice on lesser trains, *Century* diners rode with their kitchens at the rear against the possibility of smoke and food odors being wafted backward by the train's progress. Sleeping cars, however, traveled back and forth forever without turning because on *The Century* all room space had to face in the Hudson side of the tracks with corridors on the north or blind side, scenically speaking. This infallible rule made the cutting up and re-assembly of each train a maneuver of great complexity and multiple switching movements.

Ordinary trains were pulled into their bay at Grand Central by an electric yard engine which then stood, uncoupled, between the last car and the train gate until the train was scheduled to leave when it returned to Mott Haven at a prudent distance in its wake.

In the case of *The Century* the open observation platform with its plate glass windows and attractive interior as well as the train's name in electric lights, must be in full view of the arriving passenger and not impaired by the presence of an unsightly switcher. So, at Fifty-first Street Tower, far under Park Avenue, the train was halted as it backed down to the terminal and the switcher cut out and sent to its head end to push the cars into place for the sake of a single nice detail of what the French call *présentation*, the manner in which a fine dish is served to a restaurant patron. The *présentation* of *The Century* was always perfect.

In the lush days when railroading everywhere was rolling high and no train was more abundantly in the chips than *The Century*, its affairs were conducted with a lavishness that would freeze the marrow of today's operators. Standby locomotives were sequestered and stood facing east or west as the possibility of their being called into service required on ready tracks at Albany, Syracuse, Buffalo, Ashtabula, Toledo and Elkhart against possible failure of locomotive power, these in addition to the regular changes of engine scheduled at these points. In severe winter weather for many years a pilot engine preceded the first section westward from Buffalo to Elkhart, running on a perilously thin margin of safety and its markers often in sight of the engineer of the following train.

In the days of a 12:40 departure from Chicago when a large percentage of its eastbound passengers could be counted on to have an urgent interest in the stock market, it was the practice to send a secretary on by an earlier local train to Elkhart where he transcribed the New York closing prices from telegraphic reports and put them aboard the several sections of No. 26 as they pulled in. This function completed, he took another local back to Chicago. It was the entire extent of his duties.

The running time of *The Century* in its six decades of operations has, on numerous occasions, been changed to meet existing conditions, real or imagined. The original twenty hour schedule that had so outraged British commentators was in June 1905 cut to eighteen hours and from that time until the present has been modified in one direction or the other so often that the complete record of its timing, from 1902 to 1958 will be found in the appendix of this volume.

At least one of these changes is worthy of remark. It was the reduction in running time to fifteen and a half hours which coincided in 1954 precisely with the great proxy battle between William White and Robert Young and was designed to reinforce the incumbent management's claims to the maintenance of a very superior railroad. Once the Young interests had secured control of the property, the running time of *The Century* reverted to sixteen hours.

The carriage via *The Century's* Railway Post Office car of a great quantity of banking and commercial paper and securities dispatched directly from the sender to the train each business day in New York and Chicago was an aspect of *The Century's* operations which, among others, was an object of envious regard by officials of the Pennsylvania whose crack *Broadway* on a precisely similar schedule got only a fraction of this valuable business. From the standpoint of its contribution to the fame and prestige of *The Century*, in his close observations of this feature of *Century-Broadway* competition in the mid-twenties, John Barriger recommended that the Pennsylvania, his employer at the time, endeavor to capitalize the greater accessibility of the Hudson Terminal and Manhattan Transfer to the financial district of Wall Street than Grand Central Station and publicize among the banks and downtown business firms that precious minutes of availability could be added by sending bank and other urgent mail on *The Broadway's* R.P.O. car.

As an added inducement to the patronage of big business both in the form of head-end revenue and in passengers, Barriger suggested to his own principals that the name of *The Broad Way*, as he preferred to call it, be changed to *The Wall Street* and *The La Salle* on the westbound and eastbound sections, respectively, in order to link the Pennsylvania's train more closely with the financial communities of the terminal cities, for it was the men in these small but highly important areas who provided the major part of the prestige patronage of both trains.

None of Mr. Barriger's suggestions fell on fertile ground. The Pennsylvania felt it had already such an investment in the train's long and honorable service that it remained *The Broadway* and the banking and commercial paper of Kuhn, Loeb, The National City Bank, and Morgan & Company continued to travel by hand service to the head-end cars of *The Century* while the members of these firms and their proconsuls continued to ride in the club and sleeping cars behind. The prestige of *The Twentieth Century Limited* was simply impervious to competition.

As an indication of the amount of top priority mail handled every afternoon by *The Century*, it may be noted that the Railway Mail Service assigned several transfer clerks daily to Grand Central Station and La Salle Street to assist in the loading and cancellation of mail dispatched by the senders directly to *The Century's* mail car. Stationers in the financial districts of New York and Chicago regularly stocked red, white and blue Dennison labels reading "Via Twentieth Century," just as today they stock air mail stickers. The stickers or their equivalent imprinted by rubber stamp were a fabulous piece of advertising for the prestige of The Greatest Train in The World.

Over the years no train in the world maintained such a record for on time performance and when several sections were moving in the same direction operational procedure decreed that sections one and two arrive twelve and six minutes, respectively, ahead of time and that the third and last section pull into the train shed at exactly the scheduled arrival moment.

Annulments were infrequent for any cause, but from December 10, 1919, through December 19, both east and westbound trains were suspended in an effort to conserve fuel during a coal miners strike then afflicting the country. High speed greatly increases fuel consumption.

Like the train's running schedule the extra fare on *The Century* was subject over the years to changes and modifications suggested by the conditions of passenger business at the time. When it made its first run in 1902, the extra fare was $8.00 with a rebate of $1.00 for each hour the train might be late and a maximum refund of $4.00. In 1905 the surcharge was increased to $10.00 with a maximum refund of $6.00. Two years later the extra fare was cut to $9.00 with a maximum refund of $5.00.

Effective January 19, 1908 Extra Fare was $10.00. Refund arrangement same as above, except maximum refund $6.00.

Effective July 1, 1912 Extra Fare was $10.00. Refund arrangement as to late arrival same as above, except that maximum refund was made up to the full Extra Fare, viz. $10.00.

Effective November 24, 1912 Extra Fare $8.00. Refund account late arrival same as above, except maximum refund $8.00.

Effective August 26, 1920 Extra Fare $9.60, and refund account late arrival was based on $1.20 for each hour train was behind schedule; maximum refund $9.60.

Effective April 24, 1932 Extra Fare $10.00. No refund account late arrival.

Effective April 28, 1935 Extra Fare $7.50. No refund account late arrival.

Effective June 15, 1942 Extra Fare $5.00. No refund account late arrival.

Effective December 6, 1942 Extra Fare $3.00. No refund account late arrival.

Effective May 31, 1947 Extra Fare $5.00. No refund account late arrival.

Effective September 3, 1957 to date Extra Fare $7.50.** No refund account late arrival.

In general, during the period where refunds were made account late arrival refunds were computed as follows:

Trains arriving less than 55 minutes late were

** In August of 1957 when traffic was at an all-time low, one of the economies of the Perlman regime was to combine *The Twentieth Century Limited* and *The Commodore Vanderbilt* into a single train known as *The Twentieth Century-Commodore Vanderbilt*. During the thirty days this compromise was in effect the extra fare was suspended altogether and reverted to *The Century* when the two trains returned to separate schedules on September 19.

considered on time and no refund of any portion of the extra fare was made. Late arrivals of 55 minutes or more, but less than 1 hour and 50 minutes were considered 1 hour late; late arrivals of 1 hour and 50 minutes were considered 2 hours late, and late arrivals of 2 hours and 50 minutes were considered 3 hours late, etc.

Quite aside from its aspects as showcase for the New York Central, in which capacity *The Century's* earnings can only be surmised, the train over the years was a remarkable money maker in its own right. In 1902, the year of its inaugural, any passenger train grossing better than a dollar a mile was considered to be a paying proposition. In 1903, the first full year of revenue operations, *The Century* traveled 700,800 miles and took in $886,-000.00. The ratio rose steadily through 1905 when *The Century* earned its first yearly million, through two million in 1916 to achieve a resounding total in its banner year 1928 of $9,968,301.00. The ratio to train miles in the figure for later years is not as precise as it was in 1903 because by the time it hit its stride *The Century* usually ran in more than one section each way and these variations are not shown in the available table of operating statistics. It may nevertheless and with complete assurance be remarked that the New York Central's flagship represented an entirely satisfactory investment. Between 1902 and 1938, its gross revenue was $139,-945,364.00.

The all-time record both for numbers of sections run in a single direction and number of passengers carried by *The Century* was established on January 7, 1929 when seven sections of No. 26 brought a total of 822 passengers from Chicago for the opening of the National Automobile Show in the New York Central-owned Grand Central Palace in mid-town Manhattan. If this event was possessed of prophetic implications for the entire business of railroading, nobody seems at the time to have commented on it, but already in 1929 the motor car was casting its long shadow over the rails.

After this all-time high, fewer and fewer sections of a single train in either direction became the rule primarily because of the business debacle which set in during the fall of 1929 and also because the increasing availability of the Central's more powerful Hudson type locomotives with their greater capacity for maintaining *The Century's* schedule with heavier loads dictated the operation of fewer but longer sections.

Like everything else about the two trains, *The Broadway* for a time had its precise equivalent of *The Century's* Boston section in the form of cars originating in Washington and joining the main section of the train out of New York at Harrisburg. This service lasted from 1920 to 1923 and the Washington cars ran without the extra fare that characterized the rest of the train. The Washington-Chicago service was so well patronized that it often necessitated the running of Trains No. 28 and 29 in two sections to accommodate the traffic, and in 1923 a separate train, *The Liberty Limited* running as No. 58 and 59 was inaugurated and the separation from *The Broadway* made permanent.

The Liberty Limited as a solid Washington-Chicago luxury run flourished green-bay-tree-like until 1935 when the New York Central dealt the opposition a fatal blow by according the directly competing Baltimore & Ohio the use of its Pittsburgh & Lake Erie trackage west of Pittsburgh for the B & O's *Capitol Limited*. This strategem, an intrigue worthy of a Borgia, gave the B & O a substantial time advantage over the Pennsylvania on the long Washington-Chicago haul and placed the *Liberty* at a disadvantage compared to the *Capitol Limited*. *The Liberty Limited* came to an end in 1957 after nearly a quarter of a century of service, the victim of an assassination by the competition as subtly conceived as any by a Florentine prince of the cinquecento.

Legend, some of its items attesting the almost unearthly wonderments of its service, promptitude, safety, cuisine, equipment and the exalted nature of its clientele cluster thickly around *The Century* and may be attributed in their origin to the remarkable press the train has had over the years. The New York Central did not retain the services of Steve Hannigan, most dexterous publicist of his time, for nothing. One of them concerns the celebrated red carpet that used to be and perhaps at this writing still is rolled out at Grand Central for *The Century's* departure. It comes in two versions: one that its use was inspired by the red carpets footmen in the various Vanderbilt homes along Fifth Avenue were accustomed to spread across the sidewalk whenever a member of the family entered his carriage or automobile, a custom which only came to an end in 1942 when the last Vanderbilt mansion disappeared and Mrs. Cornelius Vanderbilt moved into an apartment. The Vanderbilt tie-in with the lofty *ton* of *The Century* was a natural. The other version is more republican in its connotations and holds that the red carpet treatment for passengers was suggested by showman S. L. (Roxy) Rothafel and that the railroad gave him a lifetime pass in payment. This redaction of the saga appeared most recently in "The Best Remaining Seats, The Story of the Golden Age of the Movie Palace." I have been unable to verify either, but certainly the red carpet was an inspired gesture that contributed measurably to the overall *eclat* of riding The Greatest Train in The World.

The first carpet used for departure of *The Century* was solid Harvard red and remained in service until the run of the special section for George Cardinal Mundelein, known as *The Cardinal's Train* to the XXVIII International Eucharistic Congress at Chicago in June 1926. The original crimson might have been entirely appropriate to the occasion except that everything, for some now obscure reason, connected with the event had to be new, and a buff runner with broad crimson borders was dreamed up by the passenger department. This remained standard until the Henry Dreyfuss streamlined train was evolved at which time a more elaborate carpet of deeper color with the train name woven into its design appeared.

Although, over the years *The Century* was the preoccupation of many annointed railroaders including the genius of its genesis, George Henry Daniels, the sustained brilliance and bravura of its performance at its zenith of splendor was largely attributable to A. H. Smith, President of the New York Central from 1913 until 1924 when he was killed, like a gentleman, by being thrown from his horse while riding in Central Park.

The on-time performance of Trains 25 and 26 was an obsession with Smith who recognized it in its true light as the most radiant imaginable advertisement and showcase of his overall operation. The record of the previous night's runs of *The Century* was on his desk on top of all other matters at the beginning of each business day, and if a particularly distinguished traveler, say Sir Thomas Lipton or the French Ambassador, had said a good

word for the train on arriving at its destination, his precise quotes were reported to the President of the Central and the day was that much easier for his subordinates.

President Smith was fond of travel and spent as much of his time as was compatible with his duties in the far and obscure places of the world. No matter if it was brought by native runner from the nearest government post in the steaming forests of India or by knee-breeched footman to the royal suite of the Hotel de Paris at Monte Carlo, the report of yesterday's *Century*, its earnings, number of passengers and names of notables, was sent by cable every day of his life to him wherever he might be. In certain circles these daily reports became privileged matter and were transmitted on a priority rating so that in the regime of the great Sir Ashley Sparks, resident manager of the Cunard Line in the United States, they went to Smith if he were at sea aboard the *Mauretania* or *Berengaria* together with the top priority company business with the captain.

Another New York Central president who rode *The Century* in preference to the fine business car No. 1 which was at his disposal was F. E. Williamson. Although it might seem that railroad travel would be fairly a commonplace in the life of the president of a great carrier, he took pleasure in the same amenities of luxury travel as he shared with other *Century* regulars: cocktails in the club car, a breath of fresh air on the open observation platform that survived into his regime, *The Century* Dinner and a long night's sleep as the train rolled tranquilly under the stars.

Once encountered on the observation platform by the author as *The Century* rocketed through the Indiana countryside to overtake and pass a long merchandise train doing a mere sixty on the adjacent track, he was asked why he didn't use his business car.

"Everything on this train is just as good as it is on my private car," he said. "And besides, I move on a faster schedule on *The Century* than on any train that can carry No. 1."

"Look at those high cars roll," he exclaimed, as we passed the head end of the swiftly moving freight. "There's nothing so beautiful in the world as a money making train going places fast on a spring evening!"

The author's experience of *The Century* was not only as a fairly regular patron in the thirties and forties, but vicariously through the agency of one of the first of the now numerous and familiar sound effect recordings of steam railroading on phonograph disks. A friend had presented me with a primordial version of this now commonplace rail buff artifact purporting to recreate on a phonograph the sounds of *The Century* complete with a train caller at Grand Central, whistles, crossing bells, engine changes at Harmon and Albany, conversations with the dispatcher and other noisy fakements of robust steam motive power.

The writer lived at the time at The Madison Hotel at the corner of Madison Avenue and Fifty-eighth Street directly under an apartment maintained and occasionally occupied when away from Albany by New York's Governor Herbert Lehman. It was sometimes our whim, late at night and usually in wine, to play this disk at its fullest volume.

The governor shortly showed signs of apprehension and finally approached Bertram Weal, managing director of The Madison, in the matter.

"Mr. Weal," he said warily, "do you ever hear anything unusual around your hotel at night, train noises for instance, as if *The Twentieth Century Limited* were going by under your window in Madison Avenue at full speed? I'm not a drinking man or subject to hallucinations or anything, but every so often late at night I get the impression this hotel has just crossed the long bridge into Albany and is slowing down for the station there."

Mr. Weal took the matter under advisal and had no great difficulty in tracing the source of the bells and whistles. It was pointed out that The Madison leases contained clauses strictly enjoining tenants from running railroad trains at speed through their apartments and thereafter the governor slept better at night.

Until the closing years of the thirties changes in the equipment assigned to *The Twentieth Century Limited* had about them a gradual evolutionary quality that derived from the elimination of individual cars as they became worn or outmoded and their places being filled with the newest thing in diners, sleeping cars or lounges. Cars of wooden construction on steel underframes, which were standard in 1902, were in time replaced by all-steel Pullmans. Arched window goth-

ic of stained glass yielded to square-cut transom glass of solid colors and finally disappeared altogether. Open section sleepers were replaced with room space in ever increasing proportions.

Cars that were withdrawn from *The Century* pool were by no means sold south or relegated to the boondocks. They were still luxury equipment only displaced from top assignment by still finer rolling stock, and *Century* cars eventually went to the *Lake Shore Limited* and the *Ohio State Limited,* sometimes to the *Wolverine* and to Boston sections of these name trains. The Boston & Albany was for many years the recipient of hand-me-down passenger equipment. The policy governing disposal of *Century* cars was maintained into the streamlined age when equipment from the 1938 Dreyfuss train was reassigned to the *Commodore Vanderbilt* after a few years in No. 25 and 26.

This was the classic, if melancholy, life pattern of all sorts of railroad equipment. The finest business car on the line when it was replaced for Presidential occupancy, went to the first or operating vice president and so on all the way down the line until the lowly branch line superintendent's official car was forever grounded to become a trackside shack of maintenance of way.

Because of this inexorable policy, there was never, until 1938, any abrupt change in the appearance of *The Century.* Equipment became heavier, trains became longer and ran in fewer sections. Motive power graduated from Atlantic type engines to Pacific, from Pacifics to Hudsons, and from Hudsons inevitably to Mohawks** and Niagaras.

**The naming of a class of motive power Mohawk that was elsewhere known as Mountain type, or 4-8-2 wheel arrangement, was a hilarious aspect of the New York Central's widespread advertising of its "Water Level Route, You Can Sleep." This slogan was directly aimed at the rival Pennsylvania's mountainous right of way over the crest of the Alleghenys, and the suggestion was implicit that not only was sleep out of the question aboard *The Broadway* and other crack equipment of the competition, but that riding it might actually be fraught with peril to life and limb. Nor was the Pennsylvania gratified with the Central's maps in its promotional literature showing the Central's route in a smooth sweep between its terminals while the Pennsylvania progressed in a jerky graph suggestive of the most uncomfortable and precipitous passage over towering mountain ranges. With "The Water Level Route" one of its prized advertising assets, the use of a "Mountain" type engine was unthinkable, and on the Central the Mountains became Mohawks.

But the overall consist of the train retained vestigial traces of the first *Century* of 1902; it began with a steam locomotive followed by head-end revenue, Pullman sleepers, club cars and diners, and terminated with the brass railed observation platform that was the hallmark of prestige in American passenger travel. No special equipment, as railroaders are pleased to designate private and business cars, ever rode in No. 25 or 26. If a Vanderbilt wanted to go to Chicago, the Vanderbilt car of the moment, *Wayfarer, Genesta, Herkimer, Idlehour* went fast and it went stylishly, but in some other train.

In the closing years of the thirties, however, change was everywhere on the rails. New lightweight metals of great tensile strength were making the traditional all-steel construction of Pullman Standard obsolete. Tight-lock couplings, rubber draft gear and roller bearing trucks were coming into use that made the stopping and starting of a train possible as a single monolithic unit instead of a loosely linked chain of cars to be activated one after the other as the slack ran out of drawbars. Air conditioning was giving a new lease of life to depression oppressed passenger travel and improved communications and methods of dispatching and train control were cutting down schedules. An overall and inclusive word was coined to describe the slimming down of railroad equipment: it was streamlining.

Mostly it was coming into effect in the West where the Santa Fe, Union Pacific, Burlington and Rock Island were inaugurating gleaming new light weight trains of stainless steel, but nearer at home and far more influential in the Central's thinking, rumor had it that the Pennsylvania was contemplating an all-new, almost revolutionary revising of *The Broadway Limited*. The new *Broadway*, it was reported was going to eliminate forever the old open section sleeping car and substitute all-room sleeping cars in an all-room car train. The open observation platform was going to be sealed in in a sort of solarium and the entire train be built as a continuity to be handled, turned and maintained as a single entity available to the addition of extra sleeping cars at the head end if necessary, but operated as an essentially fixed unit. Dormitory cars were added to the consist for the accommoda-

tion of dining car crews who now went straight through.

To meet this challenge, the New York Central placed in operation on June 15, 1938, thirty-six years after the first run of the train, an all-new *Twentieth Century Limited* operating from a pool of sixty-two cars and ten streamlined locomotives, sufficient to keep four full trains in operating service daily. The new train was carded from depot to depot in sixteen hours, the fastest schedule ever undertaken between New York and Chicago. Its color scheme was two tones of gray with blue and silver stripes with interiors of rust, blue, tan and gray in varying tones and combinations.

The public cars, lounge, observation and diners, as well as the decorative scheme in the various Pullman sleepers, had been devised by Henry Dreyfuss, a ranking industrial designer of the time who had been selected because the only other thinkable practitioner in the field, Raymond Loewy, had been commissioned by the management of the rascally Pennsylvania to do a similar job of face lifting on *The Broadway*. Dreyfuss had, two years previously, designed the Central's first streamlined train, the experimental *Mercury*, a day train on the Chicago, Detroit, Cleveland run, and while the *Mercury* hadn't been favorably compared to the Sistine Chapel, it had been an instructive sort of pilot train or dry run for *The Century*.

The new *Century*, like *The Broadway*, was an all-room train that dispensed entirely with open section berths and the press noted editorially, and with justification, that it marked the end of an era in American travel that had been the basis for much folklore, legend and countless smoking room anecdotes and music hall gags. The entire lighting system was new and extremely advanced for its time, while a new and distinctive *Century* insignia appeared everywhere on the train imprinted on the stationery, magazine binders, dishes, glassware, match covers, the uniforms of car attendants and tickets themselves. There were speedometers in the observation cars, an innovation hitherto only available on private and business cars, and murals, fanciful maps and other decorative panels made the cars cheery. There were telephones between all cars for communicating with diner or bar, and in the diners a change of linen and lighting after the last dinner had been served transformed the handsome interiors into a reasonable facsimile of a night club that was much admired by serious drinkers although no dancing was allowed. Muzak equipment conveyed dulcet tones to *The Century's* prudent revellers.

As distinctive as the rest of the train were the Hudson locomotives in their new Dreyfuss dress. Cabs and running boards were of aluminum and rod assemblies of light weight alloy steel. All axles on both engines and tenders, as well as cross heads, driving rods and valve gears ran on roller bearings and the smoke box was sheathed in demi-sphere of polished metal bisected by an aluminum fin and terminating at the pilot bar in a curved apron that gave the appearance of an armorer's casque and sallet.

All in all, the new *Century* was very splendid and its smooth operation was almost unbelievable in its approach to Rolls Royce standards of serenity in motion. The author, as a reporter at the time, had occasion to ride on one of the press runs down the Hudson together with other members of the staff of *The New York Herald Tribune.* Leaving Albany the shades were drawn and twenty miles down the line the reporters imagined themselves still to be in the depot. No least ripple marked the surface of their highballs.

Although the trains were available to enlargement, if occasion demanded, the new *Century* of 1938 was intended for operation with thirteen cars in the following order:

1st Car — Mail Baggage Car.

2nd Car — Lounge and Baggage Combine.

3rd Car — Roomette Car (17 Roomettes).

4th Car — Roomette Car (17 Roomettes).

5th Car — 10 Roomette and 5 double Bedroom Car.

6th Car — 4 Double Bedroom, 4 Compartment and 2 Drawing Room Car.

7th Car — Kitchen and Dormitory Car.

8th Car — Dining Car.

9th Car — 4 Double Bedroom, 4 Compartment and 2 Drawing Room Car.

10th Car — 10 Roomette and 5 Bedroom (Double) Car.

11th Car — 13 Double Bedroom Car.

12th Car — 4 Double Bedroom, 4 Compartment and 2 Drawing Room Car.

13th Car — Observation Car.

The Dreyfuss *Century* of 1938 remained in useful and ornamental operation throughout the war years, carrying peak loads of military and diplomatic traffic that made space on its sleepers at a premium and added years to the age of Reginald Rose, an executive specially charged with the delicate task of allotting space on No. 25 and 26 when it was in far greater request than the available equipment afforded. The Century Club late at night on the diners saw powerful whiskey doings among Naval officers of flag rank and even occasional enlisted personnel, and the military hangovers that were unloaded at La Salle Depot in the morning were stupendous.

Wartime traffic, however, profitable to the carriers, was hard on equipment for whose maintenance and repair there were few facilities and whose replacement in luxury classifications during hostilities was forbidden by Federal authority. In 1948, just a decade after the inaugural of the first streamlined train, another *Twentieth Century Limited* was placed in service. This time two complete consists were sufficient for the even then declining passenger traffic, each costing a flat $2,000,000 and Pullman-built. Although minor innovations had been incorporated in the Dreyfuss decor and car plans, the degree of difference from the antecedent equipment was minor. In 1946 steam had disappeared from *The Century* and Diesel-electric motive power now took the trains swiftly and efficiently but without anything suggesting their ancient glory between Harmon and Chicago. The wheel had come full circle and lean years were at hand.

In the year 1914 the train shed at Grand Central as depicted below at its northern end was still open to Park Avenue and passengers boarding the advanced cars were protected by T-shaped sheds over the platform. In the same year it is evident from the photograph at the right, *The Century* carried no train herald on its observation platform railing, but passengers were just as happy as they were later to become to be pictured aboard a prestige symbol in an age that had not yet invented the phrase. *(Two Photos: New York Central.)*

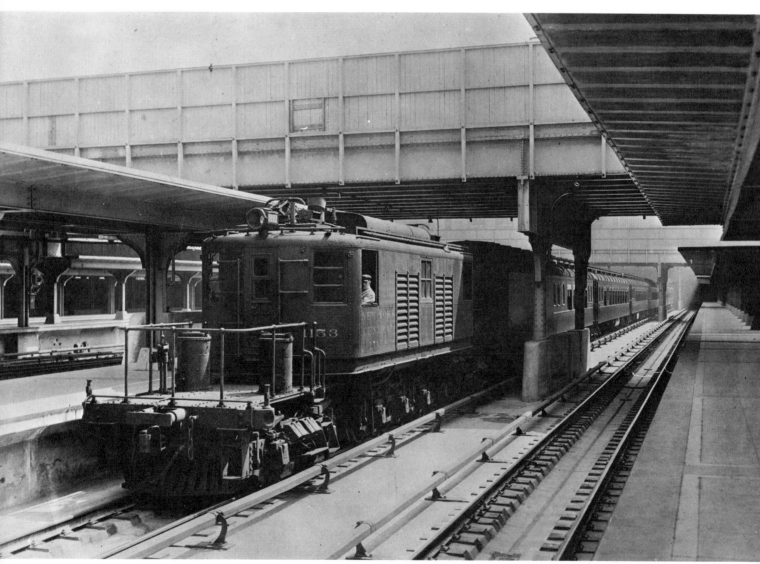

The same group that posed on the page opposite (the women are identifiable by their hats) was equally agreeable to being photographed in the club car on board the 1914 *Century*, although interior photography was then less perfect than it was to become and the car was filled with smoke from the cameraman's magnesium flare for some time afterward. *(Two Photos: New York Central.)*

In the year 1913 the panned shot in action photography was virtually unknown, which makes the above picture of *The Century* taken that year perhaps from a speed boat on the Hudson a very rare item in the iconography of railroading. It is powered by No. 3446, a light Pacific type locomotive, and the club-baggage car that rode at the head of all Trains No. 25 and 26 was one of the earlier all-steel Pullmans. The snowstorm scene below was taken at Spuyten Duyvil in 1910 with the then prevailing type of 4-8-4 electric power and the equipment is still wooden Pullman. *(Two Photos: Everett De Golyer Collection.)*

In the years before air conditioning as indicated by the fins on car windows above, much tangible wealth rode *The Century's* passenger space to complement the uncounted million in commercial paper at the head end, and among the celebrated jewels of regulars were Evalyn Walsh McLean's Hope Diamond *(left)* and Mrs. Potter Palmer's equally celebrated Palmer Pink Pearl pendant. *(Above: Everett De Golyer Collection; Below, Left: Jerome Zerbe; Right: Brown Bros.)*

Half a Century of THE CENTURY

FOR FIFTY YEARS ... "THE FAVORITE TRAIN OF FAMOUS PEOPLE."

The 20th Century Limited

WHO WAS WHO IN 1902. Many noted men and women of the day rode the original *20th Century Limited* between New York and Chicago. They included William Jennings Bryan, Booth Tarkington, Theodore Roosevelt, Lillian Russell, J. P. Morgan, Mme. Schumann-Heink, "Uncle Joe" Cannon.

WHO'S WHO IN '52. A paragraph is far too brief to call the roll of leaders in business, the professions and the arts who ride this flagship of New York Central's dreamliner fleet. For, year in, year out, daily passenger lists, prepared by the Train Secretaries on *The Century,* read like "Who's Who in America."

New York Central

The Water Level Route — You Can Sleep

Inevitably, as *The Century* entered into the national folklore and legend, it figured in the picture consciousness of the popular press. For the train's fiftieth anniversary the insertion on the page opposite appeared in *Time* suggesting the train's status as a setting for celebrities. *The Saturday Evening Post* cover shown here was painted aboard a Central diner withdrawn from *The Century* pool and spotted at Troy, New York, for the convenience of Norman Rockwell, himself a *Century* regular. The waiter is a *Century* waiter, not a professional model, while the menu on the table is a *Century* menu of the period. *(Opposite: John Barriger Collection; Above: By Permission of Curtis Publishing Company and Norman Rockwell, Abe Smith Collection. © 1946 by The Curtis Publishing Company.)*

Over the decades *The Century* rode behind a variety of motive power, each successive element of which represented, at its time of emergence, the best thinking of an aggressive and highly regarded engineering department. The locomotive type most closely associated with it in the popular mind was the long lived Hudson, a 4-6-4 wheel arrangement which might well have been named for the train itself instead of the river beside which it ran so long. Below the example of this class at the top of the page opposite, are two engines that antedated it, Atlantic type 4-4-2's built by the American Locomotive Company in 1904. No. 2999 is simple, No. 3000 a four cylinder Cole compound, and the only one of its class. Here, at the left, No. 4667 was one of the Pacifics of the twenties now downgraded to a work train where once it had powered No. 25 and below the Dreyfuss streamlining on the last of the long line of New York Central Hudsons. *(Top Opposite: Lucius Beebe; Below: Everett De Golyer Collection; Left: Robert P. Morris; Below: New York Central.)*

Mrs. Henry E. Huntington (left) widow of Collis P. Huntington who married his heir and nephew, thus keeping the Huntington wealth in the family, was strongly influenced by Lord Joseph Duveen, the international fine arts broker who helped her select furniture, old masters and her hats with fine impartiality. The Huntingtons and Lord Duveen traveled together on *The Century* and later aboard the *Aquitania* to England when Duveen purchased *The Blue Boy* for the California millionaire.

The purchase by Henry E. Huntington, through Duveen's agency, of Gainsborough's most celebrated painting from the Duke of Westminster for $620,000 was sensational news throughout the world and *The Blue Boy* arrived in New York in a tumult of publicity. To deliver the painting to Huntington in San Marino, where the magnate lived in California opulence, Duveen took space on *The Century* as far as Chicago, planning to carry the masterpiece in his stateroom with him. At the last moment, however, he remembered that he had promised to show it en route to an elderly and bed-ridden customer in Cincinnati, a Mrs. Emery, and space was switched from *The Century* to a lesser train. Lord Duveen was, however, a staunch *Century* partisan and was remembered by members of the train staff for many years as one of the most lavish of tippers. (*Huntington Library.*)

Although seven sections in a single direction might tax the availability of specific Pullman equipment, there is no record of any shortage of train heralds. This one adorns a third section out of Grand Central in the thirties. *(New York Central.)*

In his publicity booklet written for the New York Central in 1930, Edward Hungerford repeatedly asserts that all sections of *The Century* and its companion *The Advance Twentieth Century* were precisely alike in the equipment that went into the train's consist, excepting in the matter of the head end revenue car which at that time was generally run in the third New York section, a train that started light and picked up the Boston cars at Albany. An exception to this rule was the eighth section of *The Century* shown here eastbound as Train No. 26 near Albany in 1927, when it had picked up three head end revenue cars and two daycoaches for a most un-*Century*-like train indeed. When it ran in seven sections, the management sometimes lowered its usual standard of exclusive elegance and picked up miscellaneous equipment along the way, some of it deadheading in the trailing sections. The Boston train, especially when traffic was heavy, was available to non-Pullman equipment, notably reefers of perishables. *(Rail Photo Service, H. W. Pontin).*

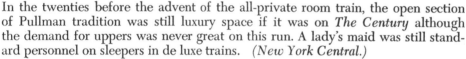

In the twenties before the advent of the all-private room train, the open section of Pullman tradition was still luxury space if it was on *The Century* although the demand for uppers was never great on this run. A lady's maid was still standard personnel on sleepers in de luxe trains. *(New York Central.)*

At the top of the opposite page, fog enshrouds three sections of *The Century* waiting on adjacent tracks for green out of La Salle depot in Chicago in 1923. In the center, below, two sections of The Greatest Train in the World are lined on parallel tracks at Grand Central, their observation compartments banked with floral tokens, to celebrate the train's Twenty-fifth Anniversary in 1927, although why the train heralds are not in place for this historic moment cannot now be determined. Still further to the right is the venerable Chauncey M. Depew, still living in the twenties, deathless legend and imperishable link with the great days when he had been the good and faithful servant of three generations of Vanderbilts. He was brought out on ceremonial occasions, like a rare and fragile piece of family plate, a long shadow out of the past who had already retired as President of the Central when *The Century* made its inaugural run in 1902. *(Three Photos: New York Central.)*

At Tower A under Park Avenue at Fifty-seventh Street, a battery of telephones against a track map of the stub lines into Grand Central symbolizes the complex train movements which daily guided *The Century* on its way between New York and Chicago and return.

Across a third of the continent, men and machines stand through the night to safeguard the passage of *The Century*. Interlocking machines such as that at Tower No. 100 at Rensselaer, New York, line the switches and set the signals at a clear board while, everywhere along the mainline, yard workers close sidings and passing tracks against the coming of The Greatest Train in The World. On the page opposite, the Albany switcher stands vigil in the cold night to cut in the Boston cars and help the train over Albany Hill and onto the long speedway across New York State where, long ago, the *De Witt Clinton* ran beside Clinton's Ditch where one day the four tracks of the Central mainline would be. *(Three Photos: Jim Shaughnessy.)*

To many and many a *Century* regular the Pullman Standard heavy steel train of the thirties was possessed of recollected comforts and conveniences in which the lighter trains, despite rubber draft gear and tight locking couplings, airflow, chromium and picture windows never came to share. There was about the equipment and the service that dominated a good, solid, secure quality of tangible workmanship that was as free from ostentation as it was freighted with durable satisfactions. The finely maintained dark green steel cars, the incredibly sleek and purposeful Hudson type engines, the cut flowers in public apartments and the beautiful table linen spoke of security and the best of everything in a well ordered world in which extra fare people got extra fare dividends of service, civility and swift assurance of transport. Mostly the decor of substantial respectability was matched by a clientele of assured substance which traveled in an atmosphere of decorous propriety that aroused impious mirth in Ben Hecht and Charlie MacArthur when they wrote "Twentieth Century." Patrons like Commander Eugene MacDonald who shot out the lights in the diner were infrequent. *(Four Photos: New York Central.)*

At the top of the page is third No. 26 behind Hudson No. 5237 crossing the Mohawk River just outside Schenectady in the year 1929. Typical of the third section which picked up the Boston cars for delivery to the Boston & Albany at Albany is the Railway Post Office which is shown running ahead of the inevitable combine buffet car which ran in all sections of *The Century*. (*Rail Photo Service: H. W. Pontin.*)

At the left, two sections of *The Century* pull in along side of each other to change engines at Harmon, New York, in the mid twenties, and the rear brakeman on the first section at the right waves green for its departure. Above the observation platform on its track at Grand Central Station in New York in 1925 is a setting and frame for feminine fashions of the moment with the legendary crimson carpet reaching into the distance at the left. (*Two Photos: New York Central.*)

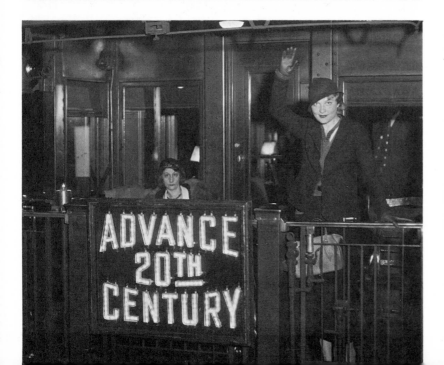

In the great days of five and six regular sections of the conventional *Century, The Advance Twentieth Century* was endowed with every aspect of luxury and prestige that characterized the older train. Names that made news rode it in equivalent density as is attested at the left where, from top to bottom, Gloria Swanson, George Arliss and Dudley Digges and Anna Sten all bore witness to the devotion of the stage and screen to the *Advance Century* as a status symbol. The Union News Company's man appeared for its sailing with periodicals appropriate to a clientele compounded of equal proportions of stage and screen, finance, industry, the professions and society in its various redactions ranging in degree from the names that appeared in Walter Winchell to those whose perfumed persons were mentioned only in Howard White's "Personal Intelligence" column in the *Herald Tribune.* (Three Photos: New York Central.)

Mindful that prestige also attached to the realm of ideas as well as to material accomplishment and acquisition, the Central's photographer was at pains to take Henry Goddard Leach, a name high in the ranks of contemporary intellectuals as an author and educator. *The Advance Century* got the same red carpet treatment *(below)* as was accorded the later sections, but occupied but a single bay in Grand Central and sailed in one section only. *(Two Photos: New York Central.)*

Regular *Century* patrons, familiar with the train's operation, regarded the run in electric power from Grand Central to Harmon much as passengers on Atlantic liners regarded the trip down New York harbor to the open sea beyond Ambrose, as a sort of preliminary to the real run of the vessel. *Century* passengers only felt themselves to be really under way when they left Harmon in steam. No. 25 is shown above skirting the Harlem River while below Spencer Tracy takes advantage of the observation car phone to make a last minute call, possibly to the boys at the bar at Bleeck's Artists & Writers Club in Fortieth Street. The phone connection was introduced at *The Century's* terminals about 1905 and was one of the extras that soon came to be taken for granted. *(Above: Everett De Golyer Collection; Below: New York Central.)*

Ordinarily the departure of *The Century* from Grand Central was a scene of well ordered decorum, as is suggested at the left, but when the run was cut to eighteen hours *(below)* the day's sailing was widely publicized and glamor derived from the presence of Mayor James J. Walker, Mr. and Mrs. William K. Vanderbilt and President F. E. Williamson. As a member of the New York State Assembly at Albany, Walker was an old accustomed patron of the train. For longer trips, although not in *The Century* consist, which never accepted special equipment, he often rode aboard publisher Paul Block's private car *Friendship.* (Two Photos: New York Central.)

At the top of the page is a stereoscopic view depicting, on the word of Underwood & Underwood who released it, "The Brotherhood of Man; William Howard Taft Greeting The Engineer of *The Twentieth Century Limited*; Copyright 1908." Skeptics may ask: "Where in the open countryside would *The Century* pause for the enactment of this fraternal scene?" Reason might suggest that the photographer, with a nice picture taken under less august circumstances, lent it prestige with *The Century's* name. Below: a customer in the club car gets the full treatment at eighty miles an hour. (*Above: Grahame Hardy Collection; Below: New York Central.*)

On the opposite page, a mood of twilight melancholy invests the Valley of the Hudson for a fine going-away panorama by a distinguished photographer of the New York Central scene, Edward L. May, who arrested *The Century* on its westward way from the rear platform of Train No. 2, *The Cayuga* in 1936. Below: action photography wasn't as perfect in 1912 as it was to become, but its very shortcomings lend a sense of speed to *The Century* on its last lap between Elkhart and Chicago in the collection of Everett De Golyer.

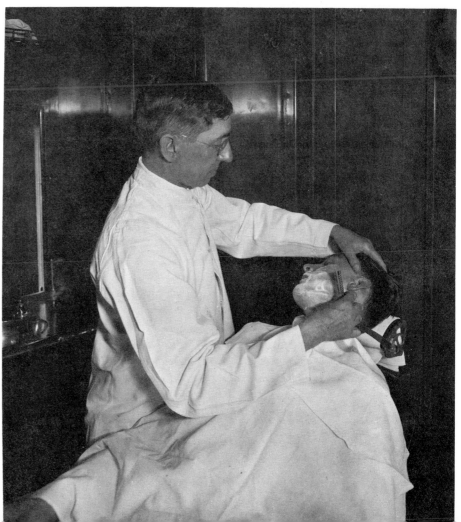

THE CENTURY DINNER

At no time, at least within the memory of living men, was the New York Central celebrated for a positively supernal excellence in its dining car cuisine. Other railroads might be of radiant repute as the abode of transcendental gastronomy; the Baltimore & Ohio from the beginning was famous for the fare on its diners, the Illinois Central to this day enjoys widespread celebrity for its lush Creole dishes and their sumptuous service, and the Santa Fe, through the agency of Fred Harvey, brought civilization to the Southwest in the form of quail in aspic, oceans of creamery butter and waitresses of resolute virtue most of whom married uncommonly well.

On the 156 dining cars it maintained at the apex of its traffic in passengers, the Central ordained a reign of creditable sufficiency, and nobody had to leave table hungry or ill-served on the *Ohio State Limited*, the *Lake Shore* or the *Wolverine*. Nobody wrote home about the food, either.

But *The Century* was different. The management emphatically believed in Cole Porter's axiom as sung by Monty Woolley to the effect that "finer things are for the finer folk," and going on the assumption that the finer folk, or most of them, rode *The Century* it undertook to provide them with the finer things.

Inevitably the diners of *The Century* would come to partake of the train's own lustrous legend but on occasion they rose above even that standard. Dinner on *The Century*, until the years of its melancholy decline, was always an experience. Sometimes it was superb.

The era that saw the birth of *The Twentieth Century Limited* also saw a new high in the material well-being of the American people and in nothing was this reflected more accurately than in their eating and drinking. Although the record is suffi-

ciently engrossed with the gastronomic activities of Diamond Jim Brady and ample ladies like Lillian Russell and Lily Langtry, it was not a time that altogether confused volume with quality and the estate of French chefs was never more honored than in such admirable restaurants as Sherry's and Delmonico's in New York, in Potter Palmer's fine hotel in Wabash Avenue and the Poodle Dog and The Palace, to name two extremes of propriety that had a common culinary meeting ground in San Francisco. In Colorado Springs, the Antlers Hotel boasted that its kitchens stood ready to prepare any classic and commonly accepted dish from the cuisine of any nation on short notice. Game was still available in North America in seemingly limitless abundance. Twenty course dinners at Newport and in Fifth Avenue stupefied the wealthy, while folk in less socially exalted brackets took the steamboats, ferries and open trolley cars to beach resorts where a strong waiter's apron filled with steamed clams was considered suitable hors d'oeuvres for one diner. The seafood consumed on those happy occasions ran into galactic figures and a vulgarism of the time, if anyone suffered from mild indisposition, was "It couldn't have been the lobster, so it must have been the beer."

A national preoccupation with good things at table found it easy to reconcile with the national preocupation with railroad travel. On board his first dining car back in 1868 George Pullman had served his guests including the reporters those twin excellences, champagne and oysters, and nobody in subsequent years was anxious to let down the standards thus established. Railroad menus commonly listed champagne and hock as suggested breakfast wines. Fred Harvey was gentling passengers on the Santa Fe's *California Limited* and at the depot restaurants strung along its mainline with roast quail, green turtle soup, jackrabbit stew and fresh venison. The dining car wine card of the Milwaukee advertised Mumm's Extra Dry at $2 a pint and forty year Otard cognac at .30 a glass. Green Chartreuse was .20 the glass.

None of this was lost upon George Henry Daniels, primal architect of the image *The Century* was to project upon the American consciousness.

"Feed them," he said of its patrons, "as though everyone were J. P. Morgan."

This was as fixed and absolute as anything available to English speech. Mr. Morgan was himself the standard of good living. To dine as he did was tops.

Amateurs of gastronomy and things epicurean find a study of *Century* menus over the years rewarding in nostalgia and the usual subject for melancholy comparison with the present in the matter of prices.

The year 1902 when *The Century* began running was the heyday of the dollar dinner on American trains. It embraced terrapin Maryland on the Southern Railway, broiled live Maine lobster on the Boston & Maine and on a Christmas Day menu of the Chicago & North Western for those happy folk who were spared the infamies of domesticity, there appeared jackrabbit stew, ruffed Canadian grouse, filet mignon and Southdown mutton.

In this era of plenty *The Century* immediately established itself in the snob category of status symbols by raising the price of its evening meal to $1.25 which made eating aboard the cars approximately the equivalent of dining at Soulé's Pavillon in years to come. This was the age when the two-bit tip was munificent, a pint of Perrier Jouet champagne was $2.25 and a Corona Corona cigar, then an all-Havana product, was four bits, so that anyone but Diamond Jim Brady, who ate his oysters in six dozen lots, would have been hard put to it to spend more than $5 on the most bountiful repast.

Management lamentations in later years to the contrary notwithstanding, diners were never money makers on American railroads, although to hear the complaints of the carriers in hard times about their dining car losses one might imagine they had once operated in bonanza. If a steward on *The Century* at any time was able to show a return of fifty cents on every dollar it cost to operate his car, he was content and so was the management. Earnings of fifty-two cents per dollar outlay were a cause for congratulation.

Good things showered down on dining car patrons of *The Century* from the start. When the train was inaugurated in 1902 Dr. William Seward Webb, a Vanderbilt in-law and in his own right a magnifico of towering dimensions, was President of the Lake Shore & Michigan Southern over whose tracks the Central operated west of Buffalo and, until its absorption by Pullman, had been President of the Wagner Palace Carbuilding Company which built all the luxury rolling stock for the Vanderbilt lines.

In the manner of many of the rich millionaires of his generation, Dr. Webb was a gentleman farmer and also, like many of the well-to-do, he admired to make his hobbies pay off a little. On his eye-popping Shelburne Farm on the shores of Lake Champlain in Vermont Dr. Webb maintained a herd of purebred Hereford cattle and as a logical consequence nothing but Shelburne Farm butter appeared on the dining cars of *The Twentieth Century Limited*. In an age uninhibited by a consciousness of calories and when cost accountants didn't even enjoy the estate of churls to which they later achieved, the diners of *The Century* may well have rolled on butter in their journal boxes. By order of the dining car department Shelburne Farm butter was used not only for service at table but for all cooking purposes in the dining car galleys and the records show that a pound of butter per passenger per trip between Chicago and New York was standard operations.

Nor was this go-for-broke attitude limited to the condiments and accessories of dining on The Greatest Train in The World. It prevailed all down the line and, as Ed Hungerford whimsically remarked, throughout the alphabet of gastronomy from asparagus to zwieback. If Maine lobsters were in short catch for a given year, *The Century* stocked them in special abundance. In an age when out-of-season strawberries had their origin almost exclusively in Arkansas, special arrangements were made to expedite shipments from St. Louis, their point of distribution, to Chicago for breakfast on *The Century*. Lake Michigan whitefish were a specialty on the train's diner west of Buffalo and Long Island scallops on cars assigned to the run between Buffalo and New York. Freezing and flying had yet to leave their mark on the national table, and regional gastronomy was a pleasant aspect of travel. Also, in the beginning and until the mid-thirties, through diners didn't exist on *The Century* or any other New York Central runs to Chicago. They were changed at Buffalo for lines east and lines west and the menus on the two divisions always varied in detail and regional dishes.

For approximately the first thirty years of its existence *The Century* operated different dining cars on its lines east of Buffalo and those west. Separate purchasing departments and superintendents serviced and directed these as distinct operations and, in the case of *The Century* diners were cut out at Buffalo where they lay over to be incorporated in the next train in the opposite direction. This ponderous operation, rendered more complex and costly in direct ratio to the number of sections being handled on a given night, necessitated a number of switching pulls and cuts which were not always appreciated by occupants of the sleeping cars to the rear of the diners and added ponderably to the delay to the trains at stations of negligible importance in the matter of passengers originating there. The practice was already established when *The Century* came into being and had its origins in the nineties when the tonnages involved in hauling a car that was to all intents and purposes deadheading through the night was a factor in running costs of trains. The savings it represented in fuel and sometimes a double heading of motive power outweighed the inconvenience. There was also the problem of suitable sleeping quarters for diner crews.

The changing of diners east and west was for many years, however, seasonal and, beginning in mid-December and continuing until mid-February, all *Century* diners ran through to the terminals. The reason was that the cars frequently froze up at Buffalo during the layover despite the precaution of keeping them on steam lines. Frozen journals had to be thawed out and delayed trains sometimes as much as an hour and one specially bad winter frozen ferns and cut flowers cost the department $1,000 above the budget.

The character of the train underwent an appreciable change when its running time was cut to

sixteen and a half hours and it no longer left Chicago before luncheon, according to Abe Smith, for many years senior dining car steward in *The Century* pool and today the head of the Central's entire dining and sleeping car service.

"The dining car had somethng of a social cachet then," he says. "You will remember that this was before Byfield started The Pump Room and Chicago women had no focus for social contacts comparable to what they had later at the Ambassador East. We had a higher percentage of well placed women, Harveys, Fields, that sort of thing. Sometimes they lunched on the train and got off before we left La Salle or, on occasion, rode as far as Englewood and then got off. The management was of two minds about this practice. It admired to have the extra business and dining car stewards were able to point to a higher income ratio per passenger when they served a meal to people who were not really passengers, but there was always the possibility that legitimate patrons might have to wait for a luncheon table. The steward just had to use his own judgment."

A distinguished patron of *The Century* in the twenties when he was looting the art galleries of Europe and selling old masters to American archmillionaires on a scale never until then dreamed of was Sir Joseph, later Lord Duveen. Duveen, a man of Lucullan tastes and great liberalities with servants (the butler of one New York collector retired on Duveen's gratitude for such favors as making known his master's moods and table conversations in the field of Rembrandts and Romneys) was always welcome from the moment his secretary preceded him through the train gate until he got off his car in a shower of twenty dollar bills for everyone who had contributed to his comfort. Duveen, who on one occasion had tipped a deck steward on an Atlantic liner $500 to have his deck chair placed next to that of Andrew M. Mellon, felt that *The Century* was the perfect setting for a man of his unquestioned standing as the associate of really rich millionaires and, according to Edward Fowles of Duveen Brothers of New York, "often took paintings of great value with him in his stateroom" when he traveled on it.

Duveen's greatest triumph of salesmanship and procuring in the early twenties was the purchase from the Duke of Westminster of Gainsborough's celebrated "Blue Boy" and its sale for the sum of $620,000 to Henry E. Huntington, the California heir to the Southern Pacific millions of his uncle Collis Huntington and whose widow he married. The "Blue Boy" might well have been the most distinguished passenger ever to ride *The Twentieth Century Limited* in its long record of notables, for upon delivery of the painting in New York in 1921 Duveen booked passage on No. 25 to take it personally to California. At the last moment, however, he recalled that he had promised to show the masterpiece to an old and valued client who was bedridden in Cincinnati and passage on *The Century* was cancelled.

Six years later, however, on January 6, 1928, a companion painting to the "Blue Boy" called "Pinkie" definitely went out of New York with Duveen on *The Century*. On December 10, 1927, Duveen wrote Huntington that he expected the arrival of "Pinkie" in New York within a few days and, according to Fowles, he took it with him to California shortly after the turn of the year.

Abe Smith remembers Lord Duveen with special affection, not only for his liberality, which was notorious on the train, but also because he had complete faith in Smith's knowledge of his tastes and never ordered a meal but left it entirely in the hands of the dining car steward.

"I remember one trip he made with us he occupied four staterooms *en suite* in one of the *Valley* cars," Smith recalls. "There was Lord Duveen and his secretary, a special advisor or curator of some sort, a room full of paintings and four Pinkerton guards. I waited on him and asked if he cared to have the upstairs boy serve him in his room and he just looked at me blandly and said: 'Give me what I had last time.' I did, too; Lynnhavens, minute steak medium well, O'Brien potatoes, Roquefort cheese and black tea. I think there was endive salad. The guards came and ate in twos."

On another occasion Smith was assigned as steward in charge of *The Detroiter* overnight out of Michigan when Duveen unexpectedly entered the diner without warning to the staff. *The Detroiter* had no train sailing list as did *The Century* and staff members were not apprised in advance of notables aboard. Smith greeted the dealer as usual: "Good evening, Sir Joseph," and Duveen glared at him. "Lord Duveen, please!" he growled. Later

that night in the *Free Press* Smith read of his passenger's elevation in the peerage which had occurred only that day. "At breakfast I spread the Lord Duveen treatment on thick," he says. "It was good for $20 when he left the car."

Not all *Century* passengers were of Duveen's urbanity. Joseph Schenck, one of the newly rich film moguls of the period, had such bad table manners that the waiters had instructions to destroy his table linen instead of sending it to the laundry. He also had a habit of throwing tips at the waiters to see them retrieve them from the floor. They were good tips, too, usually $10. "We finally formulated a rule for the staff," says Smith. "The waiter was to thank him civilly but not reach for the money while Schenck was present. He put a foot on it and stood at attention until Schenck left the car."

For many years an identifying hallmark of *Century* cuisine was a particularly delectable pickle made of watermelon rind and served along with the olives and celery. So closely did the condiment become associated with *The Century* that once or twice when it failed of delivery or was suspended during momentary waves of economy, regulars protested in no uncertain terms and the management hastened to restore it to circulation. Research discloses that the relish is known as Old Honesty Brand and is manufactured by the Johnson-Appleby Company of Cambridge, Massachusetts, who cannot establish the date when their product was first an item of *Century* commissariat. Nor can they state authoritatively how much is used by The New York Central, but allow that they use twenty carloads of Georgia watermelon annually in its manufacture and that the largest purchasers are S. S. Pierce & Company, the ancestral Boston grocers, and the Central. It comes in eight pound tins and the number of these opened between Mott Haven and La Salle Street over the years may well be astronomical.

On the premise, perhaps, that patrons of the Boston section of *The Century* were more devoted to high thinking than to *haute cuisine*, meals on the Boston & Albany were somewhat less Lucullan. The menus for August 1933 listed a plate special for $1 that included soup, panned fresh shrimp, roast beef au jus, green apple pie and chocolate nut pudding with whipped cream, and $1.25 combinations with a choice of Cotuit oysters or vegetable soup, broiled filet of blue fish or braised chicken Creole, fig and grapefruit salad, cheese or individual strawberry shortcake. On the à la carte, Cotuit cocktail was listed at thirty cents, broiled Boston scrod, seventy cents, roast prime beef, seventy cents and fresh asparagus on toast with melted butter or Hollandaise, thirty-five cents.

The invaluable Merle Armitage whose souvenirs of *The Century* are a repository of concert hall lore *en route*, recalls good times on The Greatest Train in The World in the days of operatic giants.

"One season we were preparing to go west (says Armitage) to commence the thirty-six city tour contracted for by John McCormack, when he learned that Dame Nellie Melba, whom he knew well, would be crossing the continent on the way home to Australia. He asked Melba to take passage on *The Century* the day we were leaving for the sake of company on the overnight run to Chicago, and Dame Nellie accepted with great enthusiasm, considering her formidable hauteur.

"The party therefore consisted of Dame Nellie Melba and her maid, John McCormack, his accompanist Edwin Schneider and myself, and we occupied drawing rooms and compartments in the same car. Walking down the red carpet to *The Century* that evening, we encountered Fritz Kreisler, who was also westward bound. We invited him to join us for dinner.

"Shortly after leaving New York the dining car steward punched the bell on my apartment door, and announced that the chef was preparing a special dinner for the party, which would be served in the drawing room in just one hour. I informed all concerned, and we ordered cocktails.

"The dinner came promptly, served by smiling negroes in gleaming white uniforms, and supervised by the steward. We could scarcely have fared better at the Pavillon or the Colony. There were hot hors d'oeuvres in the true style of Sweden, Crayfish *Court-bouillon,* English Channel Sole in wine and herbs, followed by Chateaubriand and crisp salad. All with proper wines. And the dessert, served with a perfectly straight face, was, of course, Peach-Melba with a fine Tokay wine, and then the coffee. In a silver tray which came along with dessert was a note which read, COMPLIMENTS OF THE TWENTIETH CENTURY LIMITED.

"Then Kreisler, McCormack, Schneider and I retired to my compartment to discuss, over cigars, the relative merits of Amati, Stradivari and Guarnieri among the glorious violins, and the characteristics of Steinway and Mason and Hamlin pianos against those of Bechstein and Pléyel in Europe.

"An unprecedented evening which I recall with utter nostalgia, as a tribute to a train with character and personality, and a mode of travelling which was superb!"

A semi-professional admiration of railroading in general as represented by *The Century* was not uncommon in esthetic circles of a fairly long-hair order, if we may believe Merle Armitage. Jascha Heifetz, who at first scrutiny might be imagined fairly insulated from such matters as drawbar pull, tractive effort and cylinder dimensions, knew *The Century's* operating schedule with split second exactness and checked an on-schedule arrival at Harmon or lag of three minutes at East Albany on a railroad man's watch which he kept calibrated to the tolerance of error permitted in the watches of operating personnel. He never spoke of the train by name, but always professionally as No. 25 or No. 26 and displayed more savoir-faire in details of rail transport than the average traveling salesman. Armitage remembers that he spurned the conventional abode of chaos assigned to the loading of taxis at Grand Central and invariably made for the Forty-third Street exit where they were far more accessible on the Biltmore Hotel cab rank.

Igor Stravinsky had a passable working knowledge of locomotives and could maintain a creditable conversation with train crews about the relative merits, tractive effort and fuel consumption of the Central's Pacific, Hudson and Mohawk type engines as they appeared on the head end of the train over the years.

Still another musician who turned out to be a train fancier was Walter Gieseking, the pianist who was killed in an accident in London some years back. Gieseking was first of all a pianist, second a butterfly collector and after that an amateur of railroads everywhere. His two favorites were tied for first place in the *Blue Train* from Paris to the Riviera and *The Century.* He was of the opinion that the conduct of French restaurant cars with their incomparable service of a magnificent menu and the *Wagons Lits* operation of sleepers were superior to their American equivalents in railroad diners and Pullman sleepers. On his first trip aboard *The Century,* Armitage remembers, Gieseking tried to lower the window of his compartment on arrival at La Salle station in order to hand his luggage down to the porter on the platform. But if he found shortcomings in the menus and a shortage of Perrier water, Gieseking thought the overall operations and equipment of *The Century* to be tops.

"My gentleman's club in the United States is *The Twentieth Century Limited,*" he said. "It should exchange the courtesies of membership with The Travelers in Paris."

Participant in an alcoholic chapter in *The Century* saga as recounted by John O'Hara was Spencer Tracy, an actor and man of bounce whose fondness for the stuff that comes in bottles itself became legendary over the years and was never for a moment denied by Tracy himself who shunned the sanctimonious postures of fellow professionals and proclaimed it from the rooftops when he tied one on.

In the time of which O'Hara speaks, Tracy, under contract to Metro Goldwyn Mayer, had just finished a nonesuch in the company's Hollywood studios and headed for New York for the express purpose of relaxing in P. J. Moriarity's and other highly regarded outposts of Sunset Boulevard. No sooner had Tracy begun to sample things in Manhattan than the studio found to its dismay that retakes were necessary on several scenes in the recently completed film. Tracy was at length located in company with a brother of Matt McHugh, a fellow actor of convivial habit, who happened to be an employee of Loew's Inc., the theater chain. MGM got McHugh on long distance and intimated that it would be most grateful if he could persuade Tracy to return on the first available section of *The Century* and, knowing that it would be difficult, placed at McHugh's disposal the resources of their New York office.

An endproduct of these resources was a bottle of Jack Daniels from which a judicious amount of the dew of Tennessee had been removed and a liberal sleeping potion of chloral hydrate inserted in its place. It was to be given Tracy at the train gate to insure his getting all the way to Chicago where other agents of Metro would take over. The studio wanted to take no chances that Tracy might

remember friends at Albany or Buffalo. The plan worked to perfection in every detail save one: Tracy insisted that McHugh join him in his stateroom on Car 250 in an attack on the bottle before train time, where the accomplice, in the full knowledge that he too was being drugged, was forced to keep pace, drink for drink, with his intended victim. As *The Century* pulled out McHugh tottered toward Vanderbilt Avenue, only pausing to sit down on the wide marble steps for a nap. The station police took a dim view of this departure from decorum and when Tracy arrived in Los Angeles refreshed and rested, McHugh was in the tank on the Island working off a five day drunk sentence.

Neither O'Hara nor anybody else was ever able to determine the moral of this tale.

When Harry Hansen was literary editor of *The Chicago Daily News,* a post in which he followed Henry Sell, he recalls going to New York twice a year on his business occasions but only eastbound aboard *The Century.* "I had money to burn when starting out," he recalls, "but getting back to Chicago was another matter. I had spent all in the lobster palaces of Broadway and came back to work on *The Lake Shore Limited.* In an upper."

Once emplaced as a member of the Hearst hierarchy, Sell, like other executives on the payroll of San Simeon did occasional errands for W. R. not of an altogether editorial nature. One of these was to accompany Marie, Duchess de Gramont to California in the capacity of courier and general manager of her entourage. "The only duchess I had known until then," he says, "was in 'Alice in Wonderland,' and I was vastly impressed. We got to Chicago in style on *The Century,* of course, but it was grim from Chicago west. This was 1921 and *The Chief* hadn't been invented. The duchess wasn't particularly impressed with whatever train we did take, nor was she impressed with Marshall Field's where she went shopping on the way. She claimed she never saw so much absolute trash so beautifully displayed.

"Mostly she was disappointed in the attire of train staffs in America. She was used to the *Wagons Lits* waiters on the *Blue Train* who still wore white satin knee breeches and crimson tailcoats with ruffled cuffs and shirtfronts and I had trouble explaining to her that this would be viewed askance in Albuquerque. Fred Harvey had trouble enough getting the customers to wear neckties."

Most of the bibliography and reference files of *The Century* during the first fifty years of its operations is in terms of adulation and flattery. There must have been complaints from the customers but they are lost to posterity, buried in the reports of dining car stewards and the operations department at 466 Lexington Avenue. The train's press was not merely good, it was resounding. Clarence Barron, publisher of *The Wall Street Journal* and Samuel Pepys of his generation of bearded tycoons, became effusive at the train's mention. Christopher Morley gave it space in his column "The Bowling Green" in unstinted measure. So did Bennett Cerf in his widely syndicated columns. *The New Yorker* files turn up a not too profound piece in 1934 called simply "The Train" by reporter Morris Markey, and E. B. White contributed to the matter of *The Century* with the poem published in its entirety elsewhere in this volume. White's verses originally appeared in F. P. Adams' column, "The Conning Tower" in the old *New York World* and were subsequently reprinted in book form.

Mrs. E. B. White alone contributes a sour note to the swelling symphony of praise of everything connected with *The Twentieth Century Limited*.

"Are you going to write any mention of the *Twentieth Century's* manicurists?" she says. "If so, one of them is indelibly impressed on my memory because the manicure she gave me on a trip from Chicago to New York in 1929 gave me a painful finger infection and caused me to lose a fingernail!"

William I. Nichols, at one time one of the deans of Harvard College and later editor of *This Week* magazine recalls receiving spiritual aid and guidance from the cloth aboard *The Century* sometime in the early twenties when he was still an undergraduate at Cambridge. As a representative student or in some other praiseworthy capacity, Nichols had been summoned to Chicago to address an alumni group and was vainly attempting to learn his speech from notes in the club car of the the Boston section of No. 25 when, across the aisle, he spied the family clergyman. The Rev. Dr. John Rowland of the Church of the Saviour on Brook-

lyn Heights, New York, had christened the boy Nichols some years previous and they naturally fell into converse.

"Do you make many speeches," enquired the man of God when apprised of his friend's mission.

"No, sir, this is the first one I ever made, and I'm rattled," said the student.

"Then I will tell you a secret I have practiced for many years before every sermon I have ever preached," said the old gentleman. "After the doxology and when I have mounted to the pulpit, I pause for a moment and run my eye over the congregation left to right, noting as I do so the most formidable men or women present, the ones most likely to be critical of me. As I do so, I say to myself 'Go to hell!' 'You go to hell, too' and 'You, sir, may go straight to hell for all I care.' It's amazing how it gives me a sense of superiority. Then I go on with my sermon and undertake to save their souls."

Nichols, since that day a public speaker of long standing, has always attributed his success to this technique.

Throughout *The Century's* many decades as the preferred train of the great and powerful of the world, it also carried a number of corpses of distinction in the realm of society and finance whose heirs and executors felt it appropriate for the dead to travel in the same style to which they had been accustomed in happier times. Corpses traveled under the same tariff regulations as the living, one first class ticket and passage in the sleepers behind for an accompanying custodian, but with this exception: there was no extra fare for the dead. This, the management felt, was only suitable as a final courtesy to old customers who, on other occasions, had paid a surcharge to ride The Greatest Train in The World.

Occasionally corpses and consternation ruled jointly at Grand Central as on the occasion of Mary Boland's mother. Miss Boland's mother, a stage mother of Maybelle Webb dimensions, inopportunely chose to die during the Broadway run of "Jubilee," a Cole Porter musical in which the ample comedienne was a starred performer. For reasons of sentiment it was essential that Mother be buried in Hollywood and arrangements were made for Miss Boland's place on the stage to be taken by an understudy while she made a hasty trip to the Coast via *The Century* and *The Chief,* the fastest possible combination in a day before planes.

Shortly before train time, Miss Boland accompanied by Clifton Webb and several other friends arrived from The Plaza where they had been solacing the bereaved in the manner approved in crises of emotional stress since time immemorial. Miss Boland was high in alcoholic content and low in spirits. She wept in Niagaras as the party approached the underground grotto in the depot where the departed waited as in an anteroom to eternity. In the center of the grim chamber was a solitary casket enclosed in the conventional traveling shell with brass handles and raised on a catafalque. Miss Boland threw herself on top of the coffin with passionate sobs of "Mother."

At that moment a door opened and two attendants from the undertaker's rolled in a precisely similar box and Miles Bronson, the terminal manager who accompanied it, announced brightly: "That's not Mother, Miss Boland! Here comes Mother now!"

It was a moment of anticlimax over which Mr. Webb, himself an accomplished trouper, prefers to draw the veil.

Although nothing in the record of *The Century* would seem to approximate the grandeur of a club of English gentlemen whose members at stated intervals put on full evening attire to dine in stupefying magnificence on the restaurant car of the *Penzance-Aberdeen Express* where a single impediment to the complete gastronomic superlative obtruded itself because the decanting of vintage port was impractical on a moving vehicle, there was a less formal group that more or less regularly rode *The Century* simply for the ride. The six or eight members of The Twentieth Century Limited Associates made a practice of ascertaining from the management when two or three staterooms *en suite* were to be vacant as far as Albany and occupying them to that point where they disembarked and took the Albany night sleeper back to Manhattan. Canapes and cocktails were served in the observation car, according to Rogers Whitaker, the group's prime mover, after which an elaborate collation was spread in their private suite, usually with a selection of vintages that transcended the train's limited wine list. The members each and every one during the trip visited the barber shop for a cere-monial trim which was part of the ritual and as a group they paid an equally ceremonial visit to the Albany Railroad Y.M.C.A. to read the notices on the bulletin board before turning homeward.

Aside from the exclusive junketings of the train *aficionados,* Whitaker felt that *The Century,* in the thirties anyway, was "rather like El Morocco: luxurious and boring. For years on end you'd see the same Hollywood people and by the time you'd been with them all the way from Los Angeles on *The Chief* you were pretty tired of them."

That, quite aside from deals in the more tangible commodities of commerce, matters of great pith and moment in the artistic world were conducted in *The Century's* drawing rooms is attested by Merle Armitage's carefully documented minutes of a meeting in which he and Samuel Insull, perhaps the most miserable and deservedly detested of the criminal millionaires of an infamous era in American finance, were the principal participants.

Insull, an unconscionable pyramider of paper fortunes whose own career came to an end when the law caught up with him after the most ignominious flight from justice since that of Boss Tweed and brought him home to a jail cell in the Chicago he had alternately patronized and pillaged, interested himself in grand opera on the shore of Lake Michigan to a point where he was arbiter of the affairs of the Chicago Opera Company and fancied himself as a sort of Lorenzo of the town's slaughterhouse society. Chicago opera had hitherto been underwritten in the grand manner by the McCormick family, but in the twenties the McCormicks retired with the gratitude of the community and Insull, whose paper fortunes were then in the ascendency, bought his way into a position of authority that had been created by his betters. His first move was to force every singer contracted to appear in Chicago to invest according to his capacity in various Insull enterprises thus contriving a liberal rebate on any salaries he might pay from every name performer except Mary Garden who announced loudly in the Blackstone lobby: "The man is doomed!" and would have no more of him.

Armitage, as manager for the Los Angeles group of opera backers knew that, at the time, it was the unswerving policy of the Metropolitan in New York to allow none of its company to sing elsewhere in the United States and so, *faute de mieux* he had gained Insull's grudging permission to sign Rosa Raisa and other members of the Chicago troupe after which he went on to New York to make arrangements with the House of Ricordi to produce operas in their copyright.

On the way west aboard *The Century* he encountered Insull whose secretary asked Armitage to stop by the great man's drawing room after dinner. Without preliminaries, Insull told Armitage bluntly that he had reconsidered his permission for members of the Chicago Opera to visit California in the fall. Since Armitage and his associates had already announced their program for the season including its starred performers, this was a stunning blow.

"But Mr. Insull," protested the dismayed Armitage, "you can't do this. You have given your word and our whole season is predicated on your permission. You will wreck the pleasure of thousands of people who have already been told the details of the arrangement. You just can't do it!"

Insull's secretary, an impulsive young man, jumped to his feet and screamed, "You can't tell Mr. Insull what he can or can't do," and then rang for the train conductor.

"Put this man off the train at Buffalo," commanded Insull when the conductor appeared. "He is threatening me with bodily harm."

The conductor was obviously in a spot, but rose to the occasion with the diplomacy of a Metternich. "I put nobody off this train on your say-so or that of anybody else," he told Insull, "but I suggest that Mr. Armitage who is a regular and valued passenger with us, retire to his compartment."

At Chicago next morning Armitage got his California committee members on the phone where the decision was made to appeal to the authorities at the Metropolitan in New York, a group where Insull was known to enjoy no great esteem, and the same afternoon saw Armitage eastbound on No. 26 with the same conductor.

"I think the old man is nuts," said this worthy, off the record. "He's nothing but trouble. I think he has delusions."

"I was well aware of the reputation for hauteur enjoyed by the great Gatti-Casazza of the Metropolitan," Armitage said years later, "and didn't think we had a prayer, but when I told him my story his beard fairly quivered with indigna-

tion. Also, I think he sensed that here was the opportunity for a great gesture that would endear The Met to the entire country.

"'You may tell your principals on the word of Gatti-Casazza that they can have any artists they want from the Metropolitan list and that if there is any trouble about either salary or arrangements you refer them to me,' he told me. 'We will show this Chicago imposter who runs grand opera in the United States.'

"That is how, for the first time the West Coast was able to hear Lucrezia Bori, Jeritza, Rosa Ponselle, Louise Homer, Pons, Gigli, de Luca and Lawrence Tibbett on their home grounds. It was real cloak and dagger melodrama and its setting was *The Century*."

A few years later Insull rode *The Century* on the way to jail after a flight from justice that covered half the world and had no parallel in its details of indignity on the part of a wanted criminal.

During the years when it ran in multiple sections, *The Century* maintained a special service for the reshuffling of space allocations at the last moment to accommodate travelers who desired the pleasure or business convenience of each other's company en route but found themselves assigned to different sections of No. 25 or No. 26 as the case might be. Joan Crawford, passing Hedda Hopper's table at Chasen's, might allow that she would be going east the following Tuesday and Miss Hopper, on similar safari, would reply: "See you cocktail time on *The Century* out of Chicago," only to find at the last moment that she was in First Twenty-six and Miss Crawford was riding two trains behind her. To resolve these minor contretemps, the New York Central at both ends of the run maintained a special liaison officer or rather group of them to adjust matters to the satisfaction of all concerned. Separate functionaries were assigned to handle traffic in theatrical names, another to sports, a third to banking and another to formal society and it was the duty of these specialists to look out for the whims and preferences of notables who fell within his jurisdiction.

For many years a Mr. Reginald Rose had charge of newspaper and magazine personnel. A disembodied voice on the telephone to me, for we never met, Mr. Rose with the unfailing courtesy of a cotillion leader got me space in wartime and apprised me of professional company that might be riding with me that night. "I know you to be on good terms with Mr. Ted Patrick," he would announce. "You'll have a pleasant trip; he's in Drawing Room A, Car 256. That's the one between you and the diner."

Throughout its glory years, *The Century*, as the pride of the New York Central and its most radiant showcase, had competition direct, implacable and explicit from the rival Pennsylvania whose *Broadway Limited* on the Chicago-New York run on an overnight schedule matched that of *The Century* in every detail of timing, operation and equipment.

The rivalry was well established long before either train came into being, and had its antecedents back in the days when the Pennsylvania's Tom Scott and the Central's William Henry Vanderbilt, both personal magnificoes of resounding dimensions, regarded their respective railroads as extensions of their own personalities and conducted their affairs as participants in a prestige sweepstakes. Under Scott and his eventual successor, the enormously patrician Alexander Cassatt, the Pennsylvania Railroad was an operation of great style, run according to ruthless standards of excellence that fully justified its slogan of "The Standard Railroad of The World."

Whatever one railroad did, the other promptly duplicated and often surpassed whether it was in luxury of equipment, speedy scheduling of trains or improved operational procedure, and this razor keen competition found its apotheosis in the two crack trains of the rival carriers.

It was a race without important also-rans. Other roads, notably Erie, the Baltimore & Ohio, the Lackawanna and the Lehigh Valley maintained services between New York and Chicago over their own lines or via connecting affiliates, but they were not serious contenders in the field of express passenger traffic. The Central and the Pennsy were the true giants and they slugged it out, toe to toe, no holds barred.

But although *The Broadway Limited*, from almost any aspect of its service, maintenance and schedule was the peer of *The Century*, it never quite achieved the cachet of social desirability or panache of glamor which was associated with *The Century* from the very beginning. *The Broadway*

was a train of remarkable beauty, much of its clientele derived from Main Line Philadelphia and down the years it ran neck and neck or rather pilot to pilot bar with *The Century* but until the great downgrading of *The Century* in the fifties, when *The Broadway* began attracting the prestige clientele that *The Century* lost almost overnight, it never quite made the grade socially.

Perhaps the explanation of this circumstance lay in the incalculable prestige of the Vanderbilt name. No name in the annals of America had about it the implications of success, grandeur and wealthy aloofness of that of the descendants of the founding Commodore. The family and its affairs simply reeked of tangible excellence even after its component members began to exhibit signs of the shirt-sleeve cycle and there appeared, metaphorically, spots on the collective Vanderbilt waistcoat. *The Twentieth Century Limited* was the Vanderbilt train and its family associations persisted even after another New York Central train on the identical run was actually called *The Commodore Vanderbilt*. It is, perhaps, a subject for enquiry by a student of public psychology more profound than the present essayist.

An outsize admirer, both factually and metaphorically, of *The Century* in the twenties was Clarence Barron, bearded and sagacious old publisher of *The Wall Street Journal* and a chronicler of the financial scene of Henry Clews dimensions. Barron, who was privy to the inside of everything and on terms of intimacy with Andrew Mellon, H. C. Frick and other towering giants of Wall Street, had no need of the train's secretarial service. He traveled with his own, two of them, to whom he dictated at every moment of the working day and on into the hours other men reserved for relaxation. He once attended a performance of the "Folies Bergère" in Paris and gave alternate dictation to two secretaries throughout the evening to the incredulous dismay of the management, who were divided between awe and insult.

Barron was a fastidious epicure and his name on the train secretary's report put the chefs on the diner on their mettle. It was the great man's practice to eat his way regularly through six successive dinner suits of progressively larger size. When he got to the point where he strained his most capacious evening trousers he took the cure at Battle Creek and started all over again.

The Century never carried more than a pound of fresh Russian caviar at a time, even when it cost no more than $18, simply because the demand was limited from a clientele more minded for sirloin than sturgeon. Barron would often consume the entire train stock in his stateroom while having cocktails and dictating. In the diner he would go straight down the menu, a thing few patrons were equipped to do in an age that was increasingly calorie-conscious: relish, soup, fish, entree, salad, dessert, coffee and cigar. Upmann cigars and, after repeal, Mumm's Extra Dry, one bottle. Refreshed and combing fugitive crumbs from his beard, he then retired to his drawing room and dictated as far as Buffalo. Much of "They Told Barron" which first appeared serially in *The Saturday Evening Post* was dictated on *The Century*.

A familiar figure on No. 25 and No. 26 en route to Hollywood after his beard had become a national institution through the agency of "The Man Who Came to Dinner" was Monty Woolley. A constant prop that went everywhere with Monty was a book that he carried under his arm but was never seen to read. It was invariably a stout, scholarly tome of formidable appearance, suggesting communion on the part of its owner with great philosophers of the past, Plato or Robert Ingersoll. Woolley's intimates knew that it was hollow and concealed a flat bottle of Jack Daniels' dew of Tennessee.

Carrying one's own Jack Daniels aboard *The Century* was mandatory upon drinkers who regarded it as the True Elixir of Life and would accept no other Bourbon because of the circumstances that in 1942 when the Jack Daniels Distillery, the first and oldest in the United States, first introduced its product in miniature bottles, the Pullman Company insisted that only 100 proof whisky be carried on cars under their management. Jack Daniels is only 90 proof and doesn't manufacture a stronger spirits although Robert Motlow, president of the firm, seriously considered manufacturing a 100 proof bottling specially for the prestige accruing from having it sold on *The Century*. The immense complexity for Federal regulations finally forced the abandonment of the project although Jack Daniels was soon available on *The Broadway Limited*, the *Panama Limited* and many other prestige runs which did their own purchasing. Hence Monty Woolley, a confirmed *Century* addict and Daniels *aficionado*, had to carry his own.

The menus of *The Twentieth Century Limited* flutter from the hand like leaves from a venerable cellar book, lithographed in green and red and blue, with gold tassels, gravure and raised printing and, inevitably the likeness of the train of the year carrying green flags at the locomotive smokebox and speeding in the artist's slipstream past Bannerman's Castle or Mohawk water or under the long bridge at Poughkeepsie. There is the old style Lake Shore menu when separate diners were operated over its divisions: roast young duck, applesauce, sweetbread croquettes, peach fritters; *The Century* Dinner for 1927 ($1.50) planked fillet of lake trout, broiled calves sweetbreads, individual chicken pot pie; there is the souvenir menu to mark the inaugural of sixteen and a half hour service, September 29, 1935; genuine Russian caviar on toast, roast ribs of prime, heavy beef; and earlier the same year the bill of fare for the seventeen hour run: fresh shad roe saute, Florentine, new asparagus in drawn butter; in 1939 the dinner was $1.75: poached eggs Benedict, roast baby spring lamb, princess salad; and there is the thirty-fifth anniversary run, June 15, 1937: veloute of spinach, royal squab grilled on toast, New York Central Special ice cream. The names of the dishes roll down the years amidst a faint hissing of air brakes and rippling of the water in the table decanters, a mobile altar piece to the memory of Claude Anthelme Brillat Savarin or, possibly, Chauncey Depew.

There are interludes of uncommon grandeur specially evoked for the Associated Philco Salesmen who had a section of *The Century* to themselves (roast Long Island duckling, sauce Bigarade) and the Republican National Women (grilled minute steaks, individual fresh strawberry shortcakes) and, with an overture from the Gloria Trumpeters massed on the Vatican balcony, the combined luncheon, dinner and breakfast menus of *The Cardinal's Train* to the XXVIII International Eucharistic Congress at Chicago, June 20, 1920, printed on watermarked paper by R. R. Donnelley & Sons Co., Chicago, who also print *Look* magazine from layouts carried on *The Century. The Cardinal's*

Train menu is bound in good Papal red; there is a tipped-in likeness of John Cardinal Bonzano, Papal Legate Extraordinary, and each day's menu itself is enclosed in a gold leaf border of Moresque or Byzantine design suggesting that (a) the seat of St. Peter was still located, not in Rome but at Constantinople or (b) that the printer was a member of the Greek Orthodox Church or other splinter sect.

The men of God did all right for themselves amidst the resources of the Central's commissary: Luncheon: mangoes, bisque of tomato, breaded spring lamb, cold roast beef, green apple pie a la mode; Dinner: canape of Russian caviar, pepper pot Twentieth Century, Lake Superior jumbo whitefish, maitre d'hotel, breast of fresh spring chicken with Virginia ham, chateaubriand of Kansas City beef, fresh asparagus Hollandaise, cantaloupe and camembert; Breakfast: red raspberries, country ham, sirloin steak, lamb chops, twelve kinds of eggs, French fries and hashed browns.

That gestures of an expansive and possibly expensive nature were an accepted part of *The Century's* routine until comparative modern times when individualism was supposed to have been reduced to a minimum is suggested by several interludes in Abe Smith's book of memories.

There was, for example, Commander Eugene F. McDonald, Jr., President of the Zenith Radio Corporation and an arctic explorer who lived at Syracuse and whose uninhibited frontier way of life was in no way abated by the general decorum that was associated with the Central's crack train and showpiece. An expansive and hospitable man, the Commander had done well at dinner one evening and was in a playful mood as time went on ("He lingered late at table," is Mr. Smith's prudent phrase), when the whim for a little target practice came over him. Although most *Century* patrons had long since discarded the habit of carrying firearms, not so Commander McDonald who was moved to draw a hog leg of immense proportions from his hip pocket and, with carefully selective aim, shot out six ceiling light fixtures the length of the dining car, scoring a bullseye with each of his available six cartridges. Far from being dismayed by this display of noisy virtuosity, the other diners, most of whom had also been "lingering late" at table, greeted the Commander's marksmanship

with a hearty round of applause before removing the shards of glass from their dessert and McDonald explained to an interested audience that the gun had once been the property of somebody known as Trigger Burke.

A problem to head waiters everywhere was Wilson Mizner who, during his Yukon years, had somehow contrived to so damage his palate that all food tasted cold to him unless it was scalding hot, far beyond the possibility of consumption by more normal diners. One night as No. 26 was rolling eastward back in Pullman Standard days, Mizner four times repeatedly sent back his Philadelphia pepper pot with complaints that it was cold even though on its next to last appearance it was actually boiling in the tureen. Finally the chef, tried beyond endurance and aware of the character of the patron with whom he was dealing, appeared at the Mizner table with a glowing, red hot poker which he plunged into the potage with open hearth pyrotechnics. Mizner was delighted.

Walter Chrysler, Sr., a regular on *The Century* in his years of golden affluence which were also those of prohibition, when he was about to retire for the night made a practice of ringing for Smith and asking for as many grapefruit as he might have traveling companions in his apartment. Cleaning out most of the insides of each fruit with a pocket knife, he then filled each with approximately half a pint of high proof cognac and set it aflame after the lights had been dimmed. Said it made an ideal nightcap. But Smith, who was inevitably invited to share the Chrysler bounty, as inevitably refused and so never went the length of the train in the wrong direction before getting back to his own car.

A commercial traveler of somewhat exalted status who often visited his firm's customers in Chicago and elsewhere in the West via *The Century* was Jules Glaenzer, senior salesman for the jewelers Cartier & Cie., who have been purveyors in diamonds and emeralds, tiaras and stomachers to the well-to-do for longer than the train has been running. In calling on a Cudahy or Armour, Glaenzer was often the custodian of gems valued in the hundreds of thousands of dollars, but because his person was well known in circles that might be covertly interested, his general practice was to travel unencumbered by wealth about his person

Running at eighty miles an hour on the advertised schedule over the New York Central's speedway west of Albany where once the traffic of a continent followed the route of the Erie Canal, Train No. 25, *The Twentieth Century Limited*, westbound, is pictured here by Howard Fogg in its apotheosis of glory, its motive power one of the Central's Niagaras that were the final and crowning triumph of the age of steam. The train's consist is eighteen streamlined Pullman-built cars of the Dreyfuss design of 1938, and the fireman is taking on water from the track pans at New Hamburg, New York. Fogg's painting is reproduced by permission of the owner, W. H. Miner Company of Chicago.

while the jewels rode, insured and guarded, in the messenger's safe up ahead to be reclaimed from the express office next day. It gave Glaenzer, a cheery type, more freedom of movement and conversation in the public cars than would have been possible with half a million dollars in negotiable necklaces in his pocket.

No chronicle of *The Century's* golden era of dining would be complete without mention of the two Tommys, Tommy O'Grady and Tommy Walsh (there was also, and to add confusion, Tommy Ryan, the train stenographer on alternate runs and almost as well known), who for many years were as much *Century* institutions as the watermelon relish and on-time arrival at its terminals. The two Tommys were diner stewards in the grand manner that characterized the office elsewhere in the person of Wild Bill Kurthy on the Southern Pacific and Dan Healy on the Milwaukee's *Pioneer Limited*.

The Tommys, whose last names were a source of confusion to hundreds of passengers who knew them over long periods, were genial Hibernian Ganymedes with bank teller memories and the aplomb of a Talleyrand or Metternich.

Known to intimates as "The Gold Dust Twins" for their almost constant association with wealth and prestige, the Tommys were both Chicago-born, well endowed with controlled blarney and over the years became fantastic repositories of the habits, tastes and peculiarities of the great and near great who rode their trains. They knew that Spencer Tracy liked to be awakened at five in the morning when he would consume a pot of the strongest and blackest coffee and then go back to sleep; that Marshall Field, although he was stern in commanding a single Martini and no more before dinner expected it to appear in a container holding four full size cocktails; that O. O. McIntyre drank only bottled mineral water when away from home and that Robert Montgomery despised demi tasse cups and wanted his after dinner coffee in breakfast cups. Captain Joseph M. Patterson, publisher of the New York *Daily News*, wanted to set Tommy O'Grady up in business with a luxury restaurant in New York, but O'Grady, while grateful, remained with *The Century*. Judge Kennesaw

Mountain Landis used to take Tommy Walsh to ball games with him to watch the Cubs play from the Wrigley box.

Tommy O'Grady nearly made a fortune when he bought an Irish Sweepstakes ticket which drew a favorite and a committee of his friends was formed to advise him on accepting the many offers of bids for shares in his horse. The advisory board was fairly august in its personnel: Governor Alfred E. Smith, A. D. Lasker, Martin J. Alger and the firearms-toting Commander McDonald. They agreed he should accept a certified cheque from a suppliant to be presented when the train reached New York at nine the next morning, but when the papers came on board at Albany hope went glimmering. The horse had been scratched.

When the axe fell and the general downgrading of *The Century* began with the inclusion of coaches in its until then exclusively all-Pullman consist, it was notable that the dining car service was the first and most widely deplored manifestation of the new order of things. Less distinguished food, conventional standards of service and general indifference to the once high standards of *Century* maintenance were widely reported by patrons hurrying to take their business to the still superlatively well maintained *Broadway Limited*.

In much the same way and to almost precisely the same degree the management decision to restore *The Century* to at least an approximation of its former prestige and glamor in the early sixties was just as promptly reflected in the immediate upgrading of its dining car service, the restoration of little niceties and smiling waiters emerging from the galley with the succulent viands of yore.

Abe Smith was told that once again the best was none too good for *Century* patrons and hurried off to Detroit where he purchased, as a starter, most of the prize beef exhibited at the 32nd Annual Junior Livestock Show. The difference in the times between 1902 and 1960 was demonstrated on the menu where the $1.50 dinner had once been a superlative gesture of prestige and snob appeal, the charcoal broiled 4-H Club prize sirloin steak *aux champignons*, together with the fixings carried a tab of $7.25. The patrons didn't care. The steak was just as good and maybe better.

"On burnished hooves his war horse trode;
From underneath his helmet flowed
His coal black curls as on he rode,
    As he rode down to Camelot."

No knightly valiant of Arthurian gallantry ever rode down to many-towered Camelot (by the island in the river) with more princely going than *The Century* as it passed Camelot, New York, at a cool eighty in the spring of 1938 behind a J-3a Hudson, the finest flowering of that wheel arrangement the world was ever to see, with burnished cylinder heads fresh from the shops. (*John P. Ahrens.*)

There is a school of thought among travelers and amateurs of railroading that includes the author of this brief monograph and believes that no agency of overland travel ever approached the spaciousness, luxury and good taste of Pullman Standard car construction in the all-steel age of air conditioning just before it disappeared under the impact of the light weight equipment of streamlined design. Shown here, with its well tailored occupants and the panache of fresh flowers that was a hallmark of *Century* luxury at the time, is a standard drawing room that may have been on any of the several car floor plans available to *Century* passengers in an age that took orchid corsages from Irene Hayes and caracul from Revillon Frères for granted on Trains No. 25 and 26. In this photograph the Irene Hayes orchids are represented by Miss Hayes herself and the Revillon fur by Constance Bennett. *(New York Central.)*

For nearly four decades, until the streamlined *Century* came off Henry Dreyfuss' drawing board, the brass railed observation cars of the great tradition and the grand manner rode at the end of every section of *The Century* and *Advance Century* and for many years were part of the Boston section out of Albany as well. It was part of the tradition of the train and the Central would as soon have considered dressing a *Century* conductor in golfing attire as sending out a train without an observation car. Only high speeds that tended to loosen track ballast in the slipstream and air conditioning which couldn't function with frequently opened doors did away with it. *(New York Central)*

In 1934 and as a sort of preview of the Dreyfuss streamlining that was to come, an Alco Hudson type locomotive No. 5344 was rebuilt at the Central's West Albany shops with a slipstream cowl or shroud and regularly assigned to one section of *The Century* where it is shown here leaving Chicago. The train was then still all-Pullman Standard and the engine, which for a time was named *Commodore Vanderbilt* left confusion in its wake when the train of that name was inaugurated. Essential services, such as those at the left, were identical in their performance both on *The Century* itself and *The Advance Century*. (Above: *Everett De Golyer Collection;* Below: *Owen Davies Collection.*)

The apotheosis of all that was magnificent in the operations of *The Twentieth Century Limited* at the zenith of its fortunes in the 1920s is suggested by this line drawing of First No. 26 passing Bannerman's Island in the Hudson by Harlan Hiney, made from a contemporary company photograph.

Although, over the years, *The Century* was the object of almost universal solicitude and its affairs received top priority attention throughout the New York Central organization, its most devoted patron and admirer was Alfred H. Smith, President from 1913 to 1924. No matter in what remote part of the world he might be at the moment, daily reports of the number of passengers, revenue, on time performance and prominent names on the sailing list of Trains No. 25 and 26 were cabled to him as urgently as though he were at his desk *(below)* in New York. When he was killed in an accident, the noble Alfred H. Smith Bridge across the Hudson below Albany was his memorial and, twice a day ever since, *The Century* has passed under it in perpetual salutation of one of the greatest railroaders in the record.   *(New York Central.)*

Sometimes *The Century* hardly made it out of town as is suggested by the melancholy scene at Root Street, Chicago, on the page opposite where a serious misunderstanding but no fatalities occurred in 1925. Mostly it sped on its way guided by such interlocking towers as that on the mainline at Rochester *(left)*. In the panorama depicted below, five sections are ready to roll from La Salle depot in 1929. *(Opposite and Below: Chicago Historical Society; Left: George Eastman House.)*

The open brass railed observation platform and illuminated train herald supplied for *The Century* what the life preservers of the *Olympic* and *Mauretania* supplied for Atlantic liners: the perfect setting for the news photographer to associate celebrities with their agency of travel. Names that made news and were patrons of The Greatest Train in The World in the thirties are shown at the left and included Irene Bordoni, Floyd Gibbons and Ginger Rogers. By the time Lily Pons (*above*) was photographed, the open observation platform had disappeared and the only identification of the train was in the caption and, for the very knowing, in the striping of the car which wasn't so satisfactory. (*Four Photos: New York Central.*)

While photographs like this in which the only index of speed is the green flags on the smokebox give scant satisfaction to amateurs of railroading in the grand manner who admire smoke in burning-of-Rome quantities, it is ideal in the eyes of the railroad's operating department, where undue smoke is viewed as inefficient firing and frowned upon with great frowning. This classic profile of *The Century* taken along the Hudson in the late twenties supplied the prototype for the New York Central's widely admired calendars of the period. Travelers at Christmas, the one day of the year No. 25 and 26 never ran in more than one section, found Yule decor *(right)* available in the club car amongst bottled matters at the bar. *(Two Photos: New York Central.)*

The Big Moment of the day at Grand Central: sailing time for *The Century* when rivers of expensive names and properties converge on Track 34, names that made news at luncheon at The Colony, 21 and Henri Soule's, guests lately registered at the St. Regis, chairmen of the board and participants in international cartels, luggage by Louis Vuiton, corsages by Max Schling, sable stoles by Valentina, perfume by Lanvin, men's boots by MacAfee, polo coats by Henry Poole, reputations by Cleveland Amory and aspirants for the notice of Earl Blackwell. The mighty and the witty, editors of *The New Yorker*, partners in Kuhn Loeb board the cars, hang up their Cavanaugh hats and set out their Cartier solid gold toilet sets and head for the bar cars, head end and rear end, of "The Greatest Train in The World." The Golden Journey to Samarkand, Ascot and The Field of the Cloth of Gold all rolled in one. *(Five Photos: New York Central.)*

The Twentieth Century

The Twentieth Century Limited, First Time It Has Reached City This Winter Covered with Icicles. It Forged Its Way Through the Blizzards Upstate and in the West. Mae Murray Is Pictured Standing Beside the Train.—*Caption of photograph in The World.*

THE storm king whistled from out the North
As the crack old Limited train set forth,
   With a hey nonny nonny.

The snow blew strong through the long, long night,
And settled on objects left and right,
But the Twentieth Century ploughed on through
As a limited train is supposed to do,
With Buffalo, Syracuse, Canastota,
Beneath more snow than their usual quota,
   And a hey nonny nonny.

From the chilly blast and the raging gale,
The Century gathered a coat of mail,
And through the blizzard it plunged and reared
With ice for whiskers, snow for a beard,
Through miles of sleet and hours of snowing
There was one bright thought that kept it going:
"If I get to New York in a great big hurry
"They'll take my picture with sweet Mae Murray,
   With a hey nonny nonny,
    "And a mae murray murray."

That was the trend of the Century's thought
As on through the fearful night it fought:
"I couldn't keep on through the Mohawk Valley
"For Lillian Gish or Marion Talley,
"But a blizzard to me is the veriest flurry
"If it leads to a photo with Mistress Murray,
   "With a mae murray murray."

So the Century train, with a sob and a shiver,
Continued its course down the Hudson River,
And weary from battling in storm and stress,
Pulled in and was met by the daily press,
And there, sure enough, looking warm and furry,
Was the dear little figure of Mistress Murray
Who, laying a hand on the Century's ice,
Appeared in all papers in less than a trice,
   With a mae murray murray.

Now here is a thing that I'm anxious to know
In the matter of pictures of ice and snow:
Assuming that turn-about *is* fair play,
Would photographs work in the opposite way?

Suppose Mae Murray came out of the West
With snow in her hair and ice on her chest,
With frost on her eyelid, sleet on her nose,
Could she make the Twentieth Century pose?
Would they take a picture of just those two,
Miss Murray's face all chapped and blue?
With the caption: "Girl Comes Grimly Through"?

Would the New York Central be quick to send
The cream of its trains to the side of a friend
Arriving in town all cold and shaken
And ready to have her picture taken?
   With a hey nonny nonny?

And unless they would, which I gravely doubt,
Why, what are these pictures all about?
   With a mae murray murray?

Gets Through

From "The Fox of Peapack"
by E. B. White. Copyright
1938 by E. B. White. Reprinted by Permission of Harper
& Brothers.

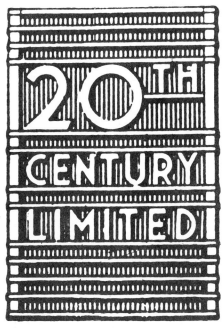

Incontestably No. 26, *The Twentieth Century*, The Greatest Train in the World, heads west behind Hudson No. 5297 under the A. H. Smith Memorial Bridge, named for one of the Central's presidents, at Castleton-on-the-Hudson in 1928. Ten all-steel Pullman Standard luxury cars and the reputation of a magnificent railroad operation ride together on the drawbar at the rear of the tender. (*Rail Photo Service, H. W. Pontin.*)

Riding the cushions on the river side of the cab, the fire boy has all the view up the Hudson from Harmon to Albany. (*Lucius Beebe.*)

Taking dictation from passengers was only part of the train secretary's job. Retrieving lost trousers for diplomats and witnessing opera contracts for Jeritza also came within his purview. *The Century* manicurists were supposed to be tops in their calling but one of them once caused Mrs. E. B. White to lose a fingernail. *(Two Photos: New York Central.)*

TWENTIETH CENTURY LIMITED

This is a memorandum of some conclusions arrived at as Madame Maria Jeritza and Mr. Merle Armitage journey westward on the Twentieth Century Limited on the evening of March 23rd, 1928. Merle Armitage has proposed that it would be thrilling and unprecedented if Maria Jeritza would sing with the opera Associations in San Francisco and Los Angles in the coming autumn. Madame Jeritza agrees.

Operas proposed and discussed would include Fedora, Tosca, Turandot and of course Carmen. Although Merle Armitage believes that no monetary compensation could adequately repay this great queen of opera for such services, he has suggested that it would be within the possibility of the theatres and their capacities, to compensate Madame Jeritza at the rate of $3,000 per performance, with four performances in each city, making a total of twenty four thoudand dollars for the season. Madame Jeritza has graciously agreed that this sum would be satisfactory.

Madame Jeritza interposes one condition. As she will be travelling without her husband, she insists that Merle Armitage meet her on her arrival in New York from Europe in September, and escort her to California. Merle Armitage accepts this commission with great honor and with extreme pleasure.

The California performances are to take place in September and October of this year, and Merle Armitage agrees to arrange the schedule so that Maria Jeritza will not be late for the opening of the rehersal period at the Metropolitan Opera House in New York.

This memoranda is a secret, personal document, between friends, and no formal contract will be executed. But Madame Jeritza gives Merle Armitage permission to announce her appearances in the newspaper and other media employed by both Associations, at their discretion.

This memorandum is signed in great mutual admiration and affection.

Maria Jeritza

Merle Armitage

Witness: Chas L. Wagner
511 Fifth Av.
New York.

Certainly one of the most remarkable memoranda of agreement in the record of grand opera is the contract reproduced opposite in which Maria Jeritza, at the time the ranking star of the opera world, agrees to appear for her agent Merle Armitage in grand opera in California. Many important contracts were undoubtedly signed aboard *The Century* in its many years as the train of the tycoons, but none as colorful as this. *(Merle Armitage Collection.)*

The aggregate seniority represented in this nightly checkup of the Pullman and New York Central conductors on a section of *The Century* came to an even 150 years of company service when the photograph was taken in 1947. From left to right are A. K. Harris, twenty-five years; M. J. O'Shaughnessy, forty-two years, A. H. Tracy, thirty-five years, and Otto C. Porcher, forty-eight years. Nobody could undertake to figure the millions of miles in rail travel this represented. *(Jesse E. Hartman.)*

In 1932 the writing team of Ben Hecht and Charlie MacArthur, whose previous fame had derived from "The Front Page," and themselves long established patrons of *The Century*, wrote "Twentieth Century," a tumultuous farce about life on the cars which was produced on Broadway by George Abbott and Phil Dunning. An instant hit with critics and theatregoers, the entire action of "Twentieth Century" was laid in a set representing one of the club cars of the period and outside the train gate in Grand Central Station. Its cast, headed by Moffat Johnson and Eugenie Leontovich, playing a demented theatrical producer and his ex-Russian mistress, respectively, a Broadway press agent directly and intentionally drawn from Dick Maney, and the stranded troupers from an Oberammergau Passion Play. Woven in a fabric of hilarious improbabilities, the play poked outrageous fun at the atmosphere of propriety which characterized the conduct of *The Century*, introduced a Passion Play Christus into the stateroom of a celebrated courtesan and generally disemboweled the haughty *ton* of the New York Central's pride and showpiece. The railroad loved it. *(Four Photos: Theater Collection, New York Public Library.)*

The two scenes of "Twentieth Century" in the club car of the train and outside the train gate at Grand Central faithfully duplicated their originals down to the last detail of Pullman decor and the attire of train crews. Here Moffat Johnson, the stricken but indomitable impresario, is being wheeled in triumph through Grand Central Depot wrapped in a clearly recognizable Pullman blanket. Railroad buffs and spies from the New York Central could detect no flaw behind the footlights.

The action of the play revolved around efforts of a flamboyant producer to induce a glamorous Russian stage star who was his discarded mistress to accept a role in a production to which she was essential. Feigning suicide, Moffat Johnson (*above*) secures her signature to the contract as the last whim of a dying man. Below, confusion ensues when the maestro's press agent mistakes his bogus suicide for a murder attempt by a religious fanatic.

The degree of realism represented by the stage sets for "Twentieth Century" fascinated New York audiences, many of whom were, of course, familiar with the train itself. In the opening scene in La Salle depot, Chicago, white porters arrived with the luggage of the principals; at the New York end of the run, as shown opposite, colored redcaps took it off. Throughout the action of the play offstage sounds faithfully reproduced the muted progress of a fast train through the darkness. In the sketch, also shown opposite, stage porters, redcaps, waiters and train crew wait their cues while at his console a sound technician imitates crossing signals and the rattle of car wheels over the track joints. The remarkable fidelity of the stage set to the interior of *The Century's* observation lounge *Elkhart Valley* may be judged by comparison of the theatrical fakement on the opposite page and the car itself as shown here. *(Opposite: Culver Service; Above: Pullman Standard.)*

For forty-five years, many of them spent in the capacity of Chief Attendant or head of the red caps, no departure of *The Century* was official without the presence of James H. Williams, a man to whom great names were a commonplace and who was on bowing terms with film stars and ambassadors, captains of finance and *grandes dames*. In the morning, too, he was on hand when No. 26 slid into its berth at Track 26 in much the same capacity as the Cunard Line's docking master supervised the arrival of *The Queen Mary*. (*Jesse E. Hartman.*)

The fact and the facsimile of *The Century's* arrival at Grand Central were indistinguishable in actuality from their recreation in the play "Twentieth Century." At the right: Train 26 is expected at Track 26. Below: Eugenie Leontovich is greeted by the press on stage at the Broadhurst Theater in the wildly successful Abbott-Dunning production of the Hecht-MacArthur farce. *(Right: New York Central; Below: Courtesy of Philip Dunning.)*

The Boston Section

With slight variations over the years the consist of the Boston *Century* closely paralleled that of the parent train in that it was always all-Pullman with an impressive proportion of non-revenue cars, a club car, diner, parlor observation and Pullman sleepers as the traffic demanded. It also carried a St. Louis sleeper out of Albany on the *Ohio State Limited* and at times its head-end revenue transcended the single mail car that rode the third section of the main *Century*. Fresh fish sometimes had the distinction of riding extra-fare as it were, Lake Superior whitefish eastbound and Maine lobsters and Cotuit oysters west, an innovation in de luxe traffic which seemed no solecism in Massachusetts whose heraldic symbol had long been a codfish.

Competition of a sort to the Boston section of *The Century* was supplied for many years by the Boston & Maine which maintained a train of many excellences including "A Wide Variety of New England Sea Food at Reasonable Prices" called *The Minute Man* on the Boston-Albany-Chicago run. *The Minute Man* called for no extra fare and ran on a far longer time card than the B & A and its sleepers went out of Albany in the *Lake Shore Limited*. A handful of diehards who viewed the Boston & Albany as a foreign corporation to be patronized only as a last resort always took the Boston & Maine, a strictly home owned and home mismanaged carrier, in preference to the subsidiary of the rascally Vanderbilts.

The alternating appearance of the names of the Boston & Albany and New York Central on equipment on the Boston run of *The Century* derived from a long standing wrangle dating back many years before the train was inaugurated. In 1887 Chauncey Depew, then President of the Central, was also a director of the B & A and a ninety-nine year agreement was signed between the carriers giving the Central access to New England over the Boston & Albany mainline and the Central in return assumed more than $5,000,000 of the New England road's obligations. Although the affairs of the Central and the B & A were thus effectively identified, New Englanders raised a storm of protest when New York Central engines and cars appeared on their once proudly home-owned railroad. The fact of foreign ownership was less offensive than its advertisement, and for years thereafter successive managements alternated in the painting of equipment nameboards. In the case of *The Twentieth Century Limited* the issue was even more confusing, since the Boston section was in fact a branchline connection with the Central at Albany. Some years the Boston section was a Boston & Albany train, others it owed allegiance to the New York Central. Its reputation for excellence was, however, constant.

The running time between Boston and Albany over the grades of the Berkshires was, over the years, approximately two hours longer than the water level run on the Central's mainline up the Hudson, and the Boston section usually was scheduled to leave that much in advance of the New York train with an appropriate cushion for switching at Albany. In 1934, when the main section of *The Century* left Grand Central at 3:15 p.m., the Boston section had left South Station at 12:45 and the two trains remade at the New York capital started over Albany Hill as one at 6:00.

In the late thirties as schedules all along the line were contracted and station stops cut to a minimum, the time lost in switching at Albany became a ponderable factor in the effective operation of a crack train and, after thirty years of showing the flag for New England, the Boston *Century* was discontinued and in its stead there appeared the streamlined *New England States.*

Boston and New England were, by this time, losing their ascendency in many aspects of American life and the proud autonomy of its institutions that had once existed was being submerged and integrated to outside influences. The passing of its own section of the greatest of all name trains, however, saddened many Bostonians. It wrote finis to an era when Beacon Street names had peopled the Boston cars as thickly as those of Murray Hill had appeared out of New York and when Mary Garden, as prima donna of the Boston Opera Company had been a frequent passenger en route to Chicago, when Major Henry L. Higginson, magnifico and patron of Boston Symphony, had accompanied the orchestra on tour to the West and the satraps of the great banking houses of State Street had smoked their Overland cigars, named for another institutional train and sold only by S. S. Pierce, the princely Boston grocers, on the observation platform.

Riverside, Massachusetts, 1938; Lucius Beebe

Depicted above is the Maiden Run of the Boston Section of *The Century* in 1909 near Riverside, Massachusetts, showing the old style banjo signals and New York Central locomotive No. 3516, which later became Boston & Albany No. 521 with four cars. Below, as it ran through the many Newtons the next day with the same motive power there were but three cars in the train's consist. *(Above: Rail Photo Service; Below: New York Central.)*

A year after its inaugural the Boston section looked like this seen from the old Cove Street bridge in downtown Boston with New York Central Pacific No. 3516 again. Below: the open observation platform of the fine Pullman built car *Proteus* was a nice place to view the Berkshire Hills on a fall afternoon. (*Above: Rail Photo Service; Below: New York Central.*)

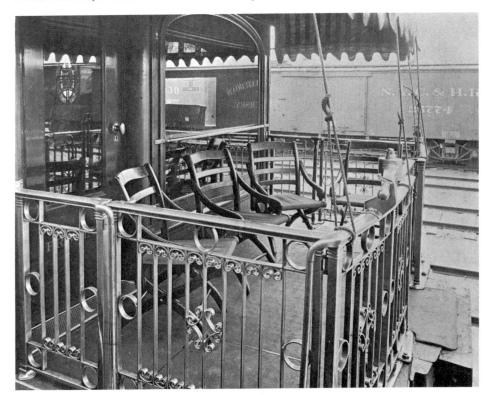

The Boston section in 1910 comprised a baggage car and four wooden Pullmans as it rolled through Riverside, Massachusetts, behind light Pacific No. 3543 bearing the insigne of the New York Central rather than the Boston & Albany on its tender. The hats in the diner were explicitly a product of R. H. Stearns & Company in Tremont Street who served all the Commonwealth Avenue carriage trade and followed the styles of Queen Mary of England. *(Above: New York Central; Below: Rail Photo Service.)*

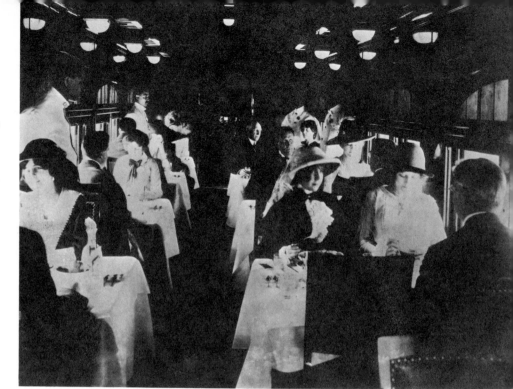

By the year 1909 Pullman interiors were noticeably plainer than when *The Century* had started its run out of New York seven years earlier and even extra fare trains still carried open section space in their sleepers. The beautiful compartment-observation car *Neponset*, assigned to the Boston section, followed Pullman practice and was named for a Boston suburb. *(Above: New York Central; Below: Pullman Standard.)*

Maine lobster, such as that being prepared here, along with Cotuit oysters, scrodded codfish and other Yankee seafood staples were, of course, regulation fare aboard the Boston section of *The Century* whose diner went as far as Albany and returned the next morning. Once in a blue moon, however, No. 25 didn't get to Albany on schedule as is suggested by the derailment depicted below of the westbound section in the summer of 1911 at Tower 10 outside of Boston when the lead Pullman split a switch. Contretemps like this were, happily, infrequent. *(Right: New York Central; Below: Rail Photo Service.)*

Until the late twenties, in any event, ladies' maids were a normal part of the train personnel of the Boston section as well as the mainline trains out of New York. Unlike stewardesses on ocean-going steamships, however, they seem to have disappeared early in the thirties, never to reappear. Whether they were victims of hard times or the growing independence of women aboard the cars who no longer required their services, the railroad is unable to say. In the frame above, No. 596 rolls the Boston section east at Faneuil, Massachusetts, on the four track mainline of the Boston & Albany in 1926, a classic study in Standard Pullman operations over a carrier of distinguished ancestry and ancient annals. (*Above: Rail Photo Service; Right: Pullman Standard.*)

The grand manner of steam railroading rode easily with the Boston section of *The Century* rolling behind No. 596, a Class K-5b Pacific on its first trip, as it passed through Faneuil, Massachusetts, with seven Pullman Standard cars on its drawbar for a date five hours later with the New York section at Albany. *(Rail Photo Service, H. W. Pontin.)*

In 1924, the Boston & Albany ordered a series of fine new Pacifics for assignment to crack passenger runs classed as K-6-A with offset smoke box door and pumps that gave them a specially racy appearance. No. 593 is shown at South Station, Boston, on its maiden run while below No. 594 surges through Faneuil with No. 26 on a zero day a few years later. *(Two Photos: Rail Photo Service, H. W. Pontin.)*

Double heading on the New York sections of *The Century* was, in later years, almost unknown east of Buffalo, but the Boston train, which had the stiff grades of the Berkshire Hills to contend with, was often powered by two locomotives all the way from Albany to Boston. The Boston cars were cut out during the dark hours at Albany from the last section of the mainline train and, at the top of the page opposite, a brakeman is giving a highball to show that the cut has been accomplished. *(Opposite: Owen Davies Collection; Below: Lucius Beebe.)*

Such elegances as monocles *(below)* on the cars of the Boston section raised no eyebrow but their owner's. *(New York Central.)*

A-1002-8

At the top of the opposite page a scene aboard the buffet of the Boston section of *The Century* in the thirties suggests that the famed individuality of the Hub rode its crack trains as well. Wine lists from the ancestral firm of S. S. Pierce and Cobb, Bates & Yerxa sluiced and gentled patrons in wing collars smoking Pierce's celebrated Overland Cigars, named for an equally famous train. Below, No. 25 at Faneuil behind No. 587 presents a fine portrait of genuine hand fired varnish in the days of Pullman Standard. Here No. 610 on No. 26 carries green for an infrequent second Boston section as it tips the summit at Charlton for the long drift downgrade into Worcester. At the right is one of the Boston train's most celebrated regulars, Clarence Barron, publisher of the *Wall Street Journal* and *Boston News Bureau* and the Samuel Pepys of American finance in his time. Many of his conversations with the captains and the kings aboard the club cars of *The Century* became history in "They Told Barron." *(Page Opposite, Top: New York Central; Below and Here Above: Rail Photo Service, H. W. Pontin; Right:* THE BOSTON GLOBE.*)*

The last run of the Boston section of *The Century* June 14, 1938. wrote the end of a notable chapter in the history of New England railroading. Here, in its last hour of glory, Train No. 25 passes through Russell. *(Rail Photo Service, H. W. Pontin.)*

When the Boston section paused at Worcester, Massachusetts, the depot campanile identified its background, while *(below)* as long as it ran the Boston train carried the proudest name in railroading on its observation Pullman. *(Above: Rail Photo Service, H. W. Pontin; Below: New York Central.)*

SULTAN AFTER SULTAN

" 'Tis but a tent where takes his one night's rest"

The status symbols of the year 1902 were somewhat different from those recognized by the generation in which the phrase itself had its origins. There were no night clubs with waiter captains to accord the accolade of recognition, no Park Avenue penthouses, no swimming pools at Bel Air, no private clubs of oil millionaires in Dallas and Houston and no picture press in which to achieve celebrity or infamy through the photographic image.

There were, to be sure, compensations for the well-to-do that established them in the general imagining and in actual fact as being well removed from *hoi polloi*. There were whole blocks of Fifth Avenue residences of palatial mein and dimension such as those of the Vanderbilt family which nested far uptown between Fifty-second and Fifty-eighth Street. There were art collections like those of Henry C. Frick, Andrew Mellon and Henry Huntington which were beginning to skim the cream of old masters from the ancestral halls of Europe and England. There were jewels like Mrs. George Gould's $500,000 pearl necklace and, soon afterward, Evalyn Walsh McLean's Hope Diamond. There were $8,000,000 cottages in Bellevue Avenue, Newport, and a growing awareness of Henry Flagler's curiously remote real estate venture called Palm Beach; there were private Pullman cars and ocean going steam yachts and boxes at The Metropolitan Opera. There were lobster palaces of gloriously baroque decor in Broadway such as Rector's, Bustanoby's and Shanley's where the menu would frighten the daylights out of today's patron of Henri Soulé or the Colony, and there were well upholstered beauties like Lillian Russell to account for raised eyebrows among the ball-fringed dowagers who clustered thickly along the porches of the United States Hotel at Saratoga in August.

The satisfactions of the year 1902 were solid like Mrs. Stuyvesant Fish's solid gold table service for 120 diners and the whisky cocktails that were such a novelty at the bar of the Manhattan Hotel in Forty-second Street. They stayed with a man like a meal for gentlemen at the Metropolitan Club that ran to twelve courses and included as a natural thing clear turtle soup, broiled lobster, terrapin, filet mignon, quail in aspic, *poire Cardinal* and Prince des Galles cigars. The perfect symbol of its durable qualities and the superlative excellence that means commanded would have been found in Rolls Royce, but in 1902 the Finest Automobile in The World was still three years in the unforeseeable future.

Into this setting *The Twentieth Century Limited* fitted without fault or flaw. It was the perfect expression of the time and spirit that gave rise to its emergence. For the convenience and occasions of personages of importance and perceptiveness it was ample in its facilities. As its celebrity and the cachet deriving from riding it became established, its dimension was enlarged to accommodate a clientele that must associate with wealth and celebrity if not actually partaking of them. Its parallel can be seen on every hand in clubs, hotels, real estate developments, fashionable restaurants. Success was part of *The Century's* passenger list from the beginning and success shortly began to strain at its seams.

An obvious customer for *The Century's* exalted financial brackets, like Bet-a-Million Gates, was Diamond Jim Brady, the steel car salesman whose wealthy ways and expensive gestures were an advertisement for his stock in trade, although I have been unable to find out how much business, if any, he did with the Central. Most of *The Century* regulars tolerated both Brady and Gates and there were a few who considered it a privilege to engage in conversation with them in the club car. Care was taken by the management, however, in the event J. P. Morgan happened to be on the same train, not to allow Jupiter to encounter these boorish vulgarians. Brady he didn't know and didn't want to; Gates he knew and explicitly despised.

One patron of *The Century* who lived up to its implications of the grand manner was Mme. Nellie Melba, the great prima donna of the time. Melba acted the part of the star performer both on stage and off and traveled in a cloud of hothouse flowers, couriers, personal attendants and the gastronomic prejudices of the well placed and determined of the world. One of her favorite dishes, plover's eggs Muscovite, hard boiled plover's eggs *en croute* with fresh caviar, she was unable to get in New York, but *The Century* lived up to her standards. Before she boarded the train, her personal staff remade her bed and toilet appointments with the diva's own specially scented bed linen and towels, and the adjacent drawing room which she used as a sitting room was decorated with Melba's own sofa pillows, silver candlesticks and a few gold framed and autographed likenesses of crowned heads for company to Chicago where she was to sing *La Bohème*. It was all approximately as Bohemian as life in Buckingham Palace.

Another magnifico who liked things to be just right and was an occasional passenger was the elder J. P. Morgan when affairs took him to Chicago. All over the world things were ordered for his pleasure so that, although he didn't go to Boston more than once or twice a year, the New Haven stocked his special brand of cigar in the club car of the *Merchants Limited,* and in his house in London, the bed was turned down and reading lamp adjusted every night, although it might be well known that he was not within 5,000 miles of London Stone. When Morgan rode *The Century* a servant from his Murray Hill home usually arrived an hour before sailing time with a bottle of the master's favorite Rhine wine which he had bought at auction in Berlin and handed it over to the dining car steward with precise directions for its chilling.

Years later the second J. Pierpont Morgan was also an occasional passenger on a later version of *The Century* that his father had patronized. He would be accompanied by his personal major domo, an attentive Scot named Bernard Stuart, who rode in an adjacent stateroom and was careful to pull down the window shades before the train passed through Ossining where Sing Sing prison was located. As the cars sped directly underneath a wing of the grim penitentiary, Mr. Morgan, in the words of Stuart, "would sigh and sigh for poor Mr. Whitney." The reference was to Richard Whitney of the New York Stock Exchange, sentenced in the thirties to serve time at Sing Sing for financial improprieties.

Over the years, the sailing lists of *The Century* came to resemble "Who's Who in America" with overtones of Burke's Peerage and Debrett, but the train's overall tone derived from Chicago. Its passenger roster glittered with Armours, Palmers, Swifts, Cudahys, Daweses, Insulls, McCormicks, Harveys and Ogdens. The commissary department went to some trouble to stock the train's diners with the commercial products, particularly in the field of hams and bacons, of the several ranking packers whose proprietors and owning families were regulars on the run. A member of the Swift dynasty, or executive in the hierarchy, or Cudahy or Armour could reasonably expect his own product along with the breakfast eggs and copy of *The Chicago Tribune* or *New York Herald Tribune* as might be indicated, but there were contretemps even so.

J. Ogden Armour on one occasion motioned an imperious fork at Harry Taggart, diner steward of the moment, as the cars were somewhere west of Elkhart and demanded to know whose ham he was being served.

"The Pride of Armour, of course, Mr. Armour," said the diplomatic Taggart.

Armour glared at his plate: "All I've got to say is that it's damned bad ham!"

A Chicago notable who was a *Century* regular and whose celebrity excused his lapses from the urbane facade encouraged by the management was Clarence Darrow. Darrow, the ranking trial lawyer of his time, was distinguished for his disregard for sartorial niceties and in later years, when he sometimes omitted to shave in the morning, his appearance was more that of an inmate of Chicago's Skid Road than of its loftier palaces of justice.

Ben Robertson, a young reporter on the staff of the *New York Herald Tribune* once was assigned to board the eastbound train at Harmon and interview Darrow, then engaged in some legal scuffle of important dimensions. Darrow usually slept with a pint under his pillow in the event of needing something in the night, and this morning he sat on the edge of his berth in haystack disarray in a seersucker coat and trousers in which, patently, the learned counsel had passed the night.

"Why, Mr. Darrow," said Robertson cheerily, "you look as though you'd been sleeping in your clothes!"

Darrow took a pull at his pint and glared menacingly at the reporter. "What the hell do you suppose I slept in?" he enquired sourly.

Another and equally un-chic occasional passenger was Heywood Broun, a columnist and sports writer for the *New York World* whose untidy appearance had so outraged General Pershing when he was a correspondent during the 1914 war that Pershing had banished him from Allied headquarters on pain of instant arrest. Broun's baggy trousers and shirt, often escaping his ample waistband, were a sartorial affront and Professor Charles Townsend Copeland of Harvard had once described him as resembling "an elephant with something on its mind."

Bugs Baer, entering the dining car one night with Grantland Rice perceived the tousled Broun at the far end of the car and suggested to Steward Tommy Walsh that perhaps a screen could be erected around the Broun table to protect the sensibilities of the other diners. Walsh refused, and Broun, learning of the projected affront, made a great show throughout dinner of attracting Baer's unwilling attention and reaching inside his shirt to scratch industriously like a monkey searching for vermin.

Such low comedy antics were foreign to the policy of *The Century* and received no encouragement from the management.

For a variety of reasons, most obvious of which was the possibility of getting off at Englewood or Harmon, as the case might be, few visitors down to see friends off ever got carried unintentionally the full distance between Chicago and New York or vice versa, a contretemps reported with hilarious frequency on trans-Atlantic liners whose North River sailings during prohibition had overtones of bacchanalia. In at least one case, however, known to the author at first hand a Gold Coast aristocrat named Jack Pierce who had been an attendant at a North Astor Street wedding saw the bride and groom off on *The Century* and continued on to New York himself. Arriving in silk top hat and morning coat, he was the first customer at Jack & Charlie's, then a speakeasy, when it opened. There he fell into conversation with an advertising executive, also smitten with the shakes, who was so charmed with him that he offered Pierce employment in his agency at a salary so attractive that the errant Chicagoan went to work for him next morning and didn't go home for two years when he again took passage on *The Century* in the opposite direction.

By the year 1916 *The Century* was so well established as a status symbol as to provide an interlude, grievous at the time, hilarious in retrospect, for Henry Sell later to become the irreproachable and august editor for *Town & Country*, itself a coated paper feuilleton of impeccable social acceptability. But in that earlier time, a youthful Sell, avid for fame and fortune, was appointed books editor of *The Chicago Daily News* or rather was told that he could call any space he could steal from other departments "The Wednesday Book Page." The stealing took place among the makeup tables one morning at five o'clock when Sell induced the makeup editor to give him the much desired billing, and that afternoon Sell purchased bedroom space on *The Century* with an eye to rustling some business among the New York publishers.

"Kind friends warned me that less expensive train passage would be more acceptable to management," Sell recalled forty-five years or so later, "but I persisted in folly, using my own money to avoid any recriminations. I was full of confidence and wanted no part of second class travel, then or now, a state of mind that has changed little with the passing years at either management or Sell level.

"Aboard the most elegant of trains, I moved to the club car where I posed as a bored sophisticate waiting the dinner hour. It came and I was conducted to an empty chair at a table for two opposite (may I use the cliche 'of all people') the owner of the *Chicago Daily News*, Mister, in every possible sense of the title, Victor F. Lawson. He made austere acknowledgment of my presence. I offered an embarrassed smile. Some moments later he cleared his throat and asked, 'We have met? I have seen your face!'

'No, Sir, we have not met, but I am Henry Sell, the new Book Page editor of your *Chicago Daily News.*'

"Lawson touched his Prince Albert beard, made a neat crescent of his moustache ends, looked out the window and spoke as to someone just over the horizon. Real cool. 'There must be some mistake. Employees of the *Chicago Daily News* do not travel on *The Twentieth Century Limited.*'

"Dinner was not easy, but somehow I managed the bouillon and creamed chicken as planned. Not hours later, although it seemed like it, but later, again the clearing of the throat . . . 'Mr. Sell, may I suggest that you try these stewed figs for your dessert. They are a little sweet but quite tasty.' A faint smile. Picking up his dinner check and mine, he paid for both and departed. As an employee of the *Chicago Daily News,* I journeyed to New York many times in years to come, always on *The Twentieth Century Limited.*"

The author of this brief profile of *The Century* used frequently to ride it on his occasions as a newspaper reporter in the New York thirties and, in his column in the *New York Herald Tribune* of the period, recorded encountering aboard it on a single westbound trip such an assortment of names that made news as Lionel Barrymore, Louis Wiley, the business manager of *The New York Times,* Gene Tunney, the Countess Dorothy de Frasso, sports writer Grantland Rice, the ranking art critic of the time, the bearded and courtly Royal Cortissoz, ex-President Herbert Hoover, Henry Sell, editor of *Town & Country,* Rufus Dawes, the Chicago banker, and the inevitable seismographic disturbance provided by the joint presence of Ben Hecht and Charlie MacArthur who had written a play about the train and were double starred celebrities with the train crew.

In the lifetime of the late Ernie Byfield, impresario of The Pump Room in the Ambassador Hotel and a dedicated collector of theatrical celebrities, *The Twentieth Century Limited* was regarded by many starring names of Broadway and Hollywood as a sort of extension of The Pump Room's ineffable gastronomy just as *The Super Chief* was regarded as an extension of Dave Chasen's legendary resort. Iced caviar with Byfield's compliments would be consigned to Helen Hayes or Ronald Coleman, care of the dining car steward, or James Cagney would find a magnum of Dom Perignon in his room when he stepped aboard at La Salle Street. Since these fringe benefits of Byfield's hospitality invariably arrived in the charge of Pump Room footmen whose silk stockings, silver buckled pumps, satin knee breeches and gold frogged liveries didn't make them precisely anonymous, everybody benefited from the ensuing *reclame.*

Once, when the author of this monograph had tarried overlong in Chicago laying waste its ordered social curriculum in the course of a transcontinental whoobab with Lady Suzanne Wilkins whose husband, Sir Hubert, was providentially under the Arctic ice cap in a submarine, Mrs. Peggy Harvey, a well placed Chicago hostess whose resources of patience and wine had been taxed, sent a singing chorus of six Western Union messengers to see him off on *The Century,* bleating, "Happy Goodbye, Mr. Beebe, Happy Goodbye To You" from the platform.

On another occasion recalled by the writer, a New York restaurateur of upper case clientele named David Cowles had represented to the Central management that he was emotionally inseparable from his two motherless puppy dogs and might he harbor the orphans in his space on the train if he would go bond for their good behaviour? In a mistaken moment of sentiment the railroad said it would be all right if the little ones could be smuggled aboard without attracting attention to their presence, and Cowles turned up with two enchanting St. Bernards whose collective weight couldn't have been less than twenty stone.

In the days before air mail was reliable and *Life* magazine was printed in Chicago, the last person through the train gates before they clanged closed every evening was one of Henry Luce's swift couriers with large flat envelopes of copy and layouts bound for Cuneo in the care of the head-end mail car. *Life's* name was engrossed in large letters on the dispatches and their urgency and the expedition of their going was lost on nobody.

On at least one occasion, the Pump Room's effulgence when translated to the train shed of La Salle Street engendered a contretemps of musical comedy dimensions. It was after Byfield's death and the affairs of the restaurant and the extension of its personality to departing trains and planes was being maintained in the bravura tradition by James Hart. The author of this monograph and his partner Charles Clegg were spotted on an adjacent track at the La Salle depot on their own private car *The Virginia City* scheduled to depart at the end of a less exalted consist than *The Century* which, neither then nor at any other time, accepted special equipment. Hart had thoughtfully dispatched a Jeroboam of Perrier Jouet to us in the care of a more than usually ornate delegation which included a waiter captain in a morning coat, two Pump Room footmen in the usual knee breeches and fourrageres and, to lend additional tone to the pageantry, a colored chauffeur in bright lavender greatcoat and top hat with a cockade.

None of the emissaries knew about private cars. They had been told to deliver the wine "to Mr. Clegg's and Mr. Beebe's car," which suggested to them its delivery to their space on *The Century*, a train with which they were familiar and where they had often completed similar missions. Told at the train gate that no such passengers were listed or expected, the Ambassador's bravos had said loudly that they knew better, they had their orders and were going on board. Our first intimation of trouble was what appeared to be an uncommonly dressy mob scene on the platform intervening between *The Virginia City* and *The Century*. Fisticuffs were being exchanged between railroad police, porters, brakemen, a large Negro in ornate attire and the decorative flunkies. In the middle of the turmoil, like a float in a Mardi Gras riot, there rose and fell perilously a vast bottle of vintage wine in a silver ice bucket. It was a scene of indescribably stylish chaos. It also fulfilled the fondest illusions of the onlookers about the conduct of life among people who owned private railroad cars. When order was finally restored and the misunderstanding explained to everybody's satisfaction, *The Century* pulled out, on time but with its staff visibly shaken.

Arthur Brisbane, for many years chief editorialist for the newspaper hegemony of William Randolph Hearst, and a cultist of eager dimensions whose favorite thesis of history was that eventually intelligent apes would take over the affairs of the world, conducted a feud of many years standing with the New York Central because of the company's refusal to stop *The Century* at Poughkeepsie where Brisbane lived. Accustomed, *ex officio*, to a certain amount of privilege especially within Hearst spheres of influence, Brisbane was miffed that the Central couldn't accommodate the schedule of their crack train to his convenience. He failed to understand the split-second rigidity of The Parade down the Hudson in the morning and up it in the late afternoon and took it as an affront that the management wouldn't set him down any nearer home than either Harmon or Albany. If intelligent apes could man airplanes, as he persistently forecast, New York Central train dispatchers could somehow figure how to make *The Century* pause in its flight. Brisbane could be relied on to assume a mood grumpy when the Central was mentioned but at least he didn't extend himself to advising the dining car to lay in a supply of Toggenburg goats, as he once suggested for all automobilists so that a constant supply of fresh milk might be always at hand.

Actually and in spite of his affected crosspatch mood, Brisbane was one of the train's most ardent supporters and admirers, giving it frequent approving mention in his syndicated columns and doing much to put it on the map of national consciousness as other newspaper columnists have done with other institutions in their favor both before and since. Brisbane's continual plugging of *The Century* vexed the Pennsylvania and John Barriger, then on the Pennsy payroll and known to have an acquaintance that extended to the great of the professional and artistic world, was asked to confront Brisbane with this scandalous partiality. Barriger did as bidden but Brisbane merely smiled his frosty smile and made mention of the phenomenal receptivity to suggestion of the apes. "Repetition is reputation," he told the discomfited Barriger, and went right on publicizing *The Century* to millions of believing readers.

It was, too, aboard *The Century* that humorist Robert Benchley, awakened at what seemed to him to be an un-Christian hour by his porter at Harmon, groped vainly on the floor of a darkened compartment for a cavalierly abandoned and now missing sock, and finally retreated to his berth in frustration muttering: "The damned thing must have gotten off at Buffalo."

Aside from Brisbane, whom the management despaired of gentling, the Central was at pains to pleasure politicians who rode *The Century* and to make them feel at home among their indisputable social betters. It was a policy that paid off in altogether tangible ways as when, during the tenure of office of the preposterous John L. Hylan as Mayor of New York, the train's departure hour was once held up for six minutes to accommodate His Honor's tardy arrival from downtown New York. Hylan was delighted and the next day a multi-million dollar suit which the City of New York was planning against the railroad in a dispute over Park Avenue taxes was quietly dropped.

"It saved us money at about the rate of a million dollars a minute," Clyde Brown, the Central's general solicitor at the time, remarked. "I figure we could hold *The Century* up to half an hour on that basis."

Although primarily she was a member of the private car club, Evalyn Walsh McLean and the Hope Diamond were occasionally on the train list traveling with her friend Cissie Patterson, the Washington newspaper publisher and member of the Chicago Patterson-McCormick clan. Mrs. McLean's weakness was not liquor, but nobody ever knew Cissie to refuse a drink, and the two old ladies smothered with cut flowers, for which Mrs. Patterson had a passion, and surrounded with tiring maids and secretaries, would hole up like a couple of Irish biddies in the state suite while a bucket brigade rushed ice from the bar and the dining room steward hovered in the corridor, menu in hand against the pleasure of one of the richest eccentrics in the record. Mrs. McLean never ventured into the public salons or diner and the management lost no sleep over the Hope Diamond. *The Century* was accustomed to tangible wealth in all its manifestations.

Alfred Lunt recalls an evening on *The Century* which, while totally devoid of significance of any sort, remains in his memory for its overtones of comedy. Traveling westbound with Lynn Fontanne in a drawing room on No. 25, they were tired, having just closed a long Broadway run of "The Visit" and were headed for home at Genesee Depot, Wisconsin, and decided to have dinner sent in. The dinner menu arrived through the agency of the tallest and blackest waiter Mr. Lunt ever remembered seeing outside a basketball team. "When he asked permission to sit down so that he could write down our order, his legs reached right into the lavatory," Mr. Lunt later recalled. "Having got our order, he pulled himself together like a folding ladder and disappeared in the direction of the diner. Half an hour later, dinner arrived as promised, but not via our boy whose reappearance we had been looking forward to as a sort of added attraction. It came by the shortest, fattest and lightest colored waiter we had ever seen, who carried it on his head with the precision of virtuosity and served it with great dexterity.

"Fascinated by the variety of sizes and shapes in which *The Century* personnel came, Miss Fontanne asked the upstairs boy about it. "Edward, he's my partner working the rooms tonight, is so thin he makes folks hungry just to look at him. I'm so fat I sort of look like an advertisement for the train's cooking. We share the tips equally, thank you, ma'am!"

Another trouper of note who played in an Anta Theater revival of "Twentieth Century" seventeen years after its rousing Broadway success and felt herself uncommonly qualified for the role was Gloria Swanson, at the time of which we write en route to Hollywood for the screening of "Sunset Boulevard." Miss Swanson was recovering from illness and her mother was traveling with her, Miss Swanson occupying a lengthwise berth in their drawing room, mother on the transverse bed, her hearing aid disconnected for the night. Miss Swanson was reading Einstein's "Science of the Universe," an unsettling sort of thing for the bedside, when suddenly she saw her feet rising above the level of her head as though gravity, obedient to Mr. Einstein, had ceased to obtain. Miss Swanson screamed as she continued to assume a perpendicular position, head down. Mother slept. Miss Swanson threw pillows at her and mother was just in time to see the berth close up almost completely on her valuable daughter. Mother grabbed the foot of the berth and tried to ring for the porter. Every time she let go to reach the night bell, the berth up-ended itself again on Miss Swanson.

When order was at length restored, it was of course apparent that the porter had failed to snap in place the restraining hook at the foot of the folding berth and that Miss Swanson's slender person had been no match for the powerful counterbalance.

"The rest of the trip was made with all my luggage piled on the foot of the berth," Miss Swanson recalls. "By the time I arrived in California I was entirely conditioned to play the neurotic Norma Desmond in 'Sunset Boulevard.'"

Although some sports writers for some reason usually preferred the less than high-church atmosphere of *The Broadway* to *The Century*, many of the top ranking newspaper sports columnists and cartoonists such as George McManus, Bugs Baer and Damon Runyon, took passage on Nos. 25 and 26. On one run W. O. McGeehan, the celebratedly acidulous sports page editor of *The New York Herald Tribune*, was passing the time of day in the club car with Gene Tunney who happened to be going West on the same train. McGeehan at the moment was conducting a one man massacre of the New York State Boxing Commission whose members he had christened "The Three Dumb Dukes" and whose chairman, the once mighty William Muldoon had been so barbarously used that he had threatened to kill McGeehan on sight. Tunney commenced to look for the exit when the burly form of Muldoon, a mighty slugger in other years, loomed in the aisle. To his surprise, however, Mc-Geehan and the aggrieved party greeted each other with glad fraternal salutations and in short order were contradicting each other with orders to the attendant for drinks. The great feud was, obviously, a canard and Tunney pondered that fights were rigged outside as well as within the boxing ring.

Bennett Cerf, a long time patron of the train who alternated commuting on the Harlem Division of the Central with the master suite on *The Century* once was assigned a compartment at the end of the car over a noisy wheel, a complaint which he promptly aired to millions of readers of his syndicated newspaper copy. The management was grieved; it wanted golden opinions of the customers, especially those with vast public communi-

cations at their disposal and gave orders accordingly. The next time Cerf's name appeared on the sailing list, the train secretary waited on him between Grand Central and Harmon with an invitation to ride the Diesel up ahead as far as Albany.

Cerf was enchanted, sat on the jump seat behind the engineer's cushions and, with the permission of that august personage, pulled the whistle cord all the way to Albany. At the capital, he climbed down from the cab and went to the diner where he joined Raymond Loewy and his wife at dinner. He was full of boyish enthusiasm for everything about *The Twentieth Century Limited*. "Isn't it a wonderful train?" he demanded of Loewy.

"Wonderful, what's wonderful about it?" snarled Loewy who hadn't been asked to restyle the Central and had seen the assignment go to an archrival in the person of Henry Dreyfuss. Loewy was on the payroll of the Pennsylvania. "It's the goddamndest train I ever rode on. Frightful color scheme, miserable lighting, simply barbarous over-all decor and it's the noisiest damn train in the world. Some childish ape was blowing the whistle all the way up the river from Harmon. Stopped now, though, thank God!"

Some idea of the density of traffic in prima donnas, opera stars and stage celebrities generally in the golden years of *The Century* is suggested by the recollections of Merle Armitage, himself a celebrated manager of musical luminaries, orchestras and ballet troupes in the first quarter of the current century.

"My earliest and most vivid impression of *The Twentieth Century Limited*," writes Armitage, "goes back to a Thanksgiving evening following a football game between Notre Dame and one of the eastern colleges, Yale, Harvard or possibly the Navy. I walked out through the concourse at Grand Central to be greeted by a sight never seen before or since. Five complete *Twentieth Century Limiteds* stood there in all their brilliance and dignity. Five observation cars with brass railings, five tail signs burning brightly, the insignia of the most famous train in the world. And five porters, their white teeth gleaming in their smiling ebony faces, directed passengers.

"The resources of a railway that could muster five complete trains with no let down in equipment, service and dining car amenities, was striking, and yet no other train on the great system suffered loss of equipment in the accomplishment. This was sometime before 1927, and since then the 20th Century has held a special place in my book.

"New York was my office, but in Chicago lived many of the stars managed by Charles L. Wagner and myself, a partnership that lasted twenty-three years. Most of these singers were members of the Chicago Opera Company, and included Mary Garden, Lucien Muratore, Alexander Kipnis, with guest appearances by our great John McCormack. And as the second largest American city, our other artists such as Walter Gieseking, Rudolph Ganz, Mischa Elman, Emmy Destinn and many more, gave frequent recitals in the city by Lake Michigan. Therefore, there was seldom a week during the opera and concert season when Wagner or I were not on *The Century* and often we made a trip or two a week. This train became our club. We were on the friendliest terms with the conductors and the porters, and of course the stewards in the dining cars always had special tables reserved, knew just how we liked our steaks, and what other favorite dishes we enjoyed. At the time, these amenities were of course appreciated and thoroughly enjoyed. But in retrospect, they stand out as the really golden years of railway travel. *The Century* was our second home, and all our great performers seemed to receive very special attention. Train crews even knew which artists were under our management, and even the haughty Mary Garden would thaw a trifle, when the steward would enquire about the health of Mr. Wagner and Mr. Armitage.

"There were many special occasions. During the year that Mary Garden was general director of the Chicago Opera Company as well as star, she included the new opera by Prokofieff, 'The Love of Three Oranges,' in the season's repertoire. Prokofieff was to come in time for the rehearsals, but through some mishap in Europe, arrived in New York only two days before the premiere performance in Chicago. The rehearsals had been in progress for weeks, but there were certain aspects of the opera which were, of course, unknown to the stars of the performance. To utilize the full opportunity to work with the Russian maestro, Mary Garden, Georges Baklanoff and Charles

Hackett came to New York and met the composer in our office.

"Almost immediately, they went to a piano in our reception room and started to untangle some of the problems which had not been indicated in the score. Garden eventually came out for some coffee and said to me, "Armitage, it's too bad there isn't a piano on the train." I immediately called the New York Central passenger traffic manager who was a friend. That night when *The Century* departed, it had an extra car in its consist, a club car in which had been placed an upright piano. This had taken some doing, as it was winter, the club car had to be brought in from the distant yards, heated, and the piano somehow inserted over the vestibule and into the car. But there it was, at train time. Garden and all the rest of the group were delighted, and worked until after midnight. Garden remembers seeing the lights of Cleveland as she retired.

"And there was the time when the Chicago Opera season closed and the orchestral scores were forgotten in the press of getting the company relocated in New York. Rushing to the Manhattan Opera House, I gathered up the music from each stand in the orchestra pit, and speeded back to the Grand Central Station. It was one minute until the scheduled departure of *The Century*, and it *always* departed on time. I hurried alongside the train until I saw a Pullman conductor and thrusting the heavy package into his astonished hands, ran along with the train to the end of the platform, explaining meanwhile that he would be met in Chicago by a very thankful assistant conductor.

"During the six years that I was a member of the Editorial Board and Art Director of *Look* magazine, we regularly shipped our daily output of layouts (type and photographs integrated) via *The Century*. Every evening our man delivered a large package to the baggage man, and the next morning a man from the printing establishment of R. R. Donnelley & Sons met the train in Chicago. It was the most reliable method of transportation of irreplaceable material we could use, for *The Century* was on time 99% of the time.

"But possibly the two most improbable memories of this train go back to the concert management days. Our great star Emmy Destinn had criticized the German Kaiser as she went through aboard *The Century* en route to her home in Prague for a summer vacation. It was at the beginning of World War I, and the Germans interned her for the duration. We had booked more than fifty concerts for this star the following fall and winter.

"By a series of curious circumstances, a strange, exotic creature came into our office in the midst of this dilemma. Intuitively, Wagner and I sensed that this unknown *might* be the replacement for Destinn. We took her to Camden, and she recorded three arias for Victor, so brilliant and lovely that we signed her that afternoon. But how to make her famous in a few months? There was no room for her at the Metropolitan, and we sent her to Chicago, where the Chicago Opera gave her a contract for two guest performances. We rented a house for this singer and her husband, and told her to stay put, and hope. One afternoon at 3 o'clock, this singer telephoned us long distance from Chicago that Campanini had scheduled her to sing *Traviata* the following night. We *must* be there. But *The Century* was booked solid. Explaining the importance of our trip to the New York Central men, they personally escorted us onto the train, explaining to the conductors that they please find some place for us to sleep. By the time we had enjoyed a fine dinner and were in Albany, the conductor discovered that someone holding a drawing room had not boarded the train and we were saved. Otherwise, they would have given us berths held for the crew!"

The performance of small courtesies by train crews in the years when America lived aboard the railroads is part of legend. The briefcase retrieved and left for the owner at Westport, the galoshes brought to New York by the club car porter of the New Haven's *Merchant's Limited* to be met at the train gate by their grateful recipient, all were more or less taken for granted as part of the comprehensive service of the carriers in an age of comparative chivalry.

That *The Century*, exalted though its destinies might be, could also fetch and carry as happily as any mixed train on the Rutland, was illustrated on one occasion when Mary Garden's personal maid forgot her jewels including diamonds she was advertised to wear next evening at a performance at the Metropolitan. Long distance identified them in the safe at the Blackstone (where else?) and the Blackstone manager in morning coat and striped trousers gave them to the Pullman conductor aboard first 26 at La Salle who gave a receipt as casually as though for a jar of cookies. Next morning the house detective and a suitable emissary from Albert Keller, the great managing director of the Ritz Carlton, was at the train gate and the transaction was reversed. Many people felt that the true New York terminal of *The Century* was the Ritz, the St. Regis or the Plaza rather than Grand Central.

Inevitably, as *The Century* became a generally recognized status symbol, travel aboard it a hallmark of worldliness and distinction. Business men in Wall Street board rooms snapped shut their hunting case watches in the afternoon and announced that it was time for them to leave if they were to catch *The Century* at six o'clock. Affluent travelers pausing for a quick one in the celebrated quadrangular bar of the Belmont Hotel just across the street from Grand Central wondered if they had time for just one more Manhattan cocktail before burrowing into the tunnel under Forty-second Street that ran directly from the Belmont bar to the train gate. As soon as the docking hour was posted, incoming passengers aboard the *Mauretania* wirelessed the porter at the Waldorf Astoria at Thirty-third Street to secure them appropriate space on the only thinkable train. In the steam room at the Yale Club stockbrokers due in Chicago in the morning peered through the mists at the electric wall clock as sailing time approached and headed for the cold showers. The Yale Club, too, had a private passageway under Vanderbilt Avenue that emerged right at the train gate.

Mention of *The Century* became an accepted topical allusion in Broadway dramas of society and highlife, and financial columnists in the daily press reported gossip overheard in *The Century* club car just as they reported hot tips "heard at the Waldorf."

Early in the nineteen thirties *The Twentieth Century Limited* became the name and central theme and setting of one of the most hilarious of all Broadway farces of the period. Charlie MacArthur, en route to join his wife Helen Hayes in Hollywood, was spending the evening doing things with bottles in the company of Ernie Byfield and

Ben Hecht in the College Inn, a grotto adjacent to the furnace room in the Sherman Hotel, and had occasion to remark on the elevated moral tone of *The Century* in which he had arrived from New York that morning.

"The club car porter wouldn't serve me White Rock for my whisky because I had kicked my shoes off and there was a hole in my sock," he complained. It was prohibition and passengers brought their own.

"I know," said Byfield. "Ethel Barrymore complained of the same thing last week. Said she threw a hard roll at John Drew in the dining car and hit an Anglican bishop. The conductor spoke to her about it."

"They wouldn't let Jesus Christ in the diner if he wasn't wearing a tie and waistcoat," said Hecht, MacArthur's collaborator in a number of disorders including a play called "The Front Page". "That gives me an idea."

Hecht and MacArthur went into a trance together a few weeks later in a suite in The Ambassador East, another Byfield Hotel where the servants were used to them, and came up with a play whose entire action was to take place aboard *The Century* eastbound and whose characters included a demented Broadway producer with delusions of grandeur, a disillusioned press agent and a Christus from a stranded troupe of Oberammergau Passion Players. The producer, a transparent synthesis of Morris Gest and David Belasco, was eventually played by Moffat Johnson with a Scotch accent opposite Eugenie Leontovich in the role of his Russian ex-mistress. The press agent was drawn to correspond with startling fidelity to Broadway's own Richard Maney, a celebrated coiner of Shubert Alley superlatives who in fact acted as press agent when "Twentieth Century" was produced by George Abbott.

The action and dialogue made infamous jape of the propriety which hung around the Central's flagship like an aura. The bearded Christus in search of employment attired in a Gethsemane suit invaded the drawing room of Moffat Johnson to exhibit his virtuosity with passages from "The Passion Play." Saul of Tarsus, also bearded like Moses, was trapped in her stateroom by Leontovich who mistakenly fancied him as a Chicago multimillionaire in search of dalliance. A religious fanatic iden-

tified with the stranded Christus pasted labels with the admonition "Prepare to Meet Thy God" on the backs of unsuspecting members of the train crew.

As the train was passing through Elyria, Ohio, in the midnight hours the harassed train conductor forsook all dignity and roared at Christus: "God's blood and blizzards, Jesus, this is *The Twentieth Century Limited!* Take off those false whiskers and that night shirt in my club car or I'll have you jailed at Buffalo!"

"Twentieth Century" was an instant and hilarious success on Broadway and only succumbed when the bank holiday darkened its marquee.

Other trains, in the golden years of travel, assumed the qualities and overtones of a private club: *The Merchant's Limited* on the New Haven, *The Congressional* on the Pennsylvania, the Milwaukee's *Pioneer Limited*. None quite so compellingly combined the membership of the Union League, Century, Lawyers, Manhattan and Coaching Clubs in their sailing list as *The Century*. John Barriger, at a time when he was a New York Central proconsul and riding *The Century* recalls that once on a single westbound section of No. 25 he encountered a sufficient number of presidents, chairmen of the board and general managers of corporations important to him to organize a dinner party with twenty guests which occupied more than half the diner when they sat down to Cotuits and Porterhouse. *The Century* over most of its long life was the best place to solicit big business.

Inevitably there is a missing trousers anecdote about the valeting department of *The Century* and, almost as inevitably, it is in an exalted realm of men's attire and concerns an ambassador. The diplomat in question was arriving on the eastbound train and was scheduled to be met at the train gate by emissaries of the State Department, a circumstance which required formal dress, since this was in a time when such amenities still obtained in the world. Finding his striped cashmere morning trousers out of press, our man gave them to the porter for pressing in the night and received the assurance they would be returned sponged, creased to a razor edge by Harmon at the latest.

Valeting was performed in the club car at the head of the train and on the morning in question, through some concatenation of mischances, the head end cars of one train were cut out at Albany and followed in another section. In car 261 consternation reigned. Telegrams thrown off at Poughkeepsie found answers at Harmon that the missing but invaluable pants were following ten miles behind their owner. The first section was due out of Harmon before Second 26 was scheduled in, but in view of the gravity of the crisis, First 26 waited, the porter of car 260 on the platform. Second 26 rolled in with the barber and pants leaning from the club car, the trousers flying in the slipstream to be retrieved as they flew past the rear cars of the waiting first section. The porter ran, the conductor highballed his train, the diplomatic magnifico donned cutaway, Ascot tie, braided edge waistcoat and missing trousers of state. At the traingate he was the mould of diplomatic form.

The Century had weathered one more crisis.

Undoubtedly, hundreds of millions of dollars worth of business contracts were signed aboard *The Century* and deals arranged running into galactic figures, but they are difficult to pinpoint and prosaic beyond the concern of posterity. One that was far from the routine cartels in steel and futures in wheat negotiated in its drawing rooms is recollected by the previously quoted Merle Armitage who, in the years when he was the foremost of all American concert agents and singers' representatives, spent so much time aboard the train as to be regarded by crews as a fixture.

In the late twenties when Maria Jeritza was the sensation of every opera house from La Scala to Covent Garden, Armitage and his associate Gaetano Merola were conducting delicate negotiations for her appearance in opera at San Francisco and Los Angeles when she had completed her current season at the Metropolitan. Jeritza's husband, the Baron Popper wanted nothing of the American West which he had heard was unsafe from Sioux war parties, but one evening after dinner at the St. Regis, the troublesome baron had retired and Jeritza told Armitage that she was vastly excited at the prospect of California and would give her professional word that she would appear there next October, but that she dared not sign a formal contract.

"I give you my solemn word and you may announce me in 'Tourandot', 'Carmen', 'Fedora' and any two others of my repertory making five in all," she told Armitage.

"I was both thrilled and dismayed (he says). Without a contract even Jeritza would not be easily acceptable to my California clients. The president of the opera in San Francisco was the late R. I. Bentley of the great Del Monte Foods company. The president of our Los Angeles company was Gurney E. Newlin, the attorney for great utility companies. Both would understand the situation, but would be very apprehensive about staking so much on a verbal agreement.

"As we said good night, Jeritza mentioned that she would like to have seen me again, but that she was going to Chicago the next day on *The Century*. 'Alone?' I enquired. 'Of course,' she replied, 'with just my two maids.' Then I asked her to have dinner with me on the train and we parted on a very happy note.

"I was very encouraged. She had held my hand as I told her of the attractions of California, and the eager and enthusiastic audiences that would greet her. She was insistent, however, that I meet her at the dock when she landed the following September 3rd on the *De Grasse* from Europe. 'I'm coming over alone, so I will need an escort for the journey west,' she explained. I replied that I had never received a more desirable assignment!

"The next afternoon as we sped up the Hudson River on *The Century's* flight to Chicago, a young man in uniform approached our table in the diner. 'Madame Jeritza and Mr. Armitage,' he said diffidently, 'are there any messages I can send or write for you?' I decided to take a bold chance. 'Come to Car 250, Drawing Room C in about an hour.' The young man nodded, and Jeritza looked hard at me. I had given him the number of her reservation. 'Why do we need *him?*' she asked. 'That young man is the secretary-stenographer on this train, and I will explain everything.' Then I went into a very carefully worded description of the American businessman's mind. Her word was certainly sufficient for *me*, but would seem a slender thread on which to hang an opera season to men not accustomed to the world of artists and performers. She was not convinced, and apparently had promised the Baron there would be no contracts. Sensing this, I reassured her that this would not be in any sense a contract, just a memorandum, which we would both sign.

"Over coffee that evening in Jeritza's drawing room, I dictated one of the most delicately worded agreements of my career. It was really a kind of love letter in which I agreed to meet her in New York and escort her to California, and she agreed to be escorted to California, and to sing five roles in San Francisco and in Los Angeles, all this of course sounding incidental to the fact that we would take *The Century* west, have luncheon at the Ambassador East, and then take *The Chief* to Los Angeles. Explaining all the amenities of the trip to her, she finally decided it was a lovely sort of memento. The young stenographer was a bright boy. He took the memo in shorthand, but he stayed right there in the drawing room and typed it on his portable. We had great fun signing our respective names with the young man's pen, and then Jeritza insisted I keep *both* copies!

"We had breakfast together the next morning as we rounded the south shore of Lake Michigan. Not a word was said about the agreement, but Jeritza was full of questions about California, and was very impressed with the fact that she would sing opposite Gigli, Schipa, Thomas and other stars, and with all our elaborate plans to receive her in the glamorous west.

"Our Boards of Directors never quite got over that memo written on the stationery of *The Twentieth Century Limited*. I had it witnessed by the stenographer before we left the train, and Newlin said it was as legal as any document he had ever inspected. There were phrases inserted in this document that Newlin observed were never before contained in any legal agreement, and he suggested it might be the basis for a whole new school of *Twentieth Century* diplomacy! It was very much enjoyed by all our directors, and *may* have had something to do with a handsome raise in my salary, which occurred at the close of the sensationally successful Jeritza opera season."

Transporting William Randolph Hearst was always something of a problem, not because he was difficult to please, which he wasn't, but because of the vast communications system that traveled with him and was a constant whether he was in residence at San Simeon, in his Riverside Avenue apartment or on the cars. A flow of messages arrived and more were dispatched all night at operational stops for, momentarily deprived of the long lines telephones, The Chief instinctively turned to Western Union. Sonny Trinidad, one of the observation car porters in the thirties, recalls that on a single westbound trip, Hearst used up the two pads of Western Union blanks in his locker and that he was obliged to send to another car for extras. Another problem was the usual presence of Marion Davies when the great man traveled. Mr. Hearst had pronounced notions about liquor, and labored under the delusion that Miss Davies almost never drank, which was strictly contrary to fact. All over the world there were secret bottles of Gordon's gin stashed with Miss Davies' name on them, in the Paris Ritz, at Claridge's in London, and in the lady's powder room at Jack & Charlie's in West Fifty-second Street and Miss Davies had access to them through the simple expedient of excusing herself from the boss, getting a couple of quick belts and returning fortified and radiant. This convenience was, of course, readily available in several oases on *The Century* and the attendants concerned learned to be expeditious in her service. Mr. Hearst became restive if she was absent too long.

That the conduct of *The Century* was looked upon as a disturbing sort of competition as well as a radiant paradigm of passenger operations by the rival Pennsylvania is a matter of constant record from earliest times when the two carriers matched the least improvement in its opposite number and *The Broadway Limited* and *The Century* slugged it out toe-to-toe for the cream of the passenger traffic between New York and Chicago.

In 1926 John W. Barriger, twenty years later to become President of the Monon and still later President of the Pittsburgh & Lake Erie and one of the outstanding authorities on the mystique of passenger transport of his generation, was on the Pennsy payroll in the capacity of Transportation Inspector. This was an office that embraced not only the close scrutiny of the practices of his own company but also the competition, especially that of the New York Central's pride and showpiece. Barriger rode *The Century* on many occasions and always with a sharp eye to its service and procedure in much the same manner a fashion spy might view the devisings of a rival couturier. He made voluminous reports to his home office on aspects of *The Century's* food, personnel, timing and equipment, and most of all upon the train's achievement of a prestige reputation.

Long before the status symbol became a part of the language, Barriger's memoranda on *The Twentieth Century Limited* revealed that the most important single contributing factor in its ascendency over the *Broadway* of the twenties was its reputation as a train which was patronized by the most enviable names in the worlds of finance, fashion and professional celebrity, and that to ride No. 25 and No. 26 was a well recognized hallmark of importance with worldwide implications. *The Century* was part of the American facade of success.

In the twenties, as it has been both before and since, name dropping was a national preoccupation. People already established in their field of ambition or endeavor as well as those on the way up the ladder were fond of casual allusions to grandeur and the rich and important names of the social and economic scene. Names who mattered lunched at the Ritz, occupied first night seats courtesy of Florenz Ziegfeld at "The Follies", addressed Otto Kahn familiarly on the bathing beach back of The Breakers at Palm Beach and spoke on terms of easy acquaintance with Texas Guinan, Scott Fitzgerald, Mayor James J. Walker or Ethel Barrymore as their ambitions might dictate. They also spoke casually about taking passage on *The Twentieth Century Limited* in much the same way they spoke of sailing with Sir James Charles in the *Aquitania* or putting up at The Broadmoor when passing through the Rockies.

A not infrequent patron of *The Century* in the days when he was being paid $1,000.00 a day in cash as a Hollywood idea man in the well heeled twenties was Gene Fowler. In the belief that there was little future ahead of the studio that employed him, Fowler insisted on being paid at the end of every business day and occasionally commuted from Chasen's to see what the boys were doing in the back room at Bleeck's in Fortieth Street, Manhattan. One of Fowler's many aphorisms to achieve immortality was: "Money is something to be thrown off the back platform of trains, preferably *The Twentieth Century Limited*."

The aura of prestige deriving from travel on *The Century* in many cases of record attracted passengers who went out of their direct line of travel to ride its cars. It was a commonplace for Saint Louisans to invoke imagined occasions to achieve New York by way of Chicago and for Philadelphians to spend a day on business or pleasure in New York before boarding No. 25 to take them westward. The latter of these evasions was a particularly galling affront to the Pennsylvania whose own *Broadway* went within easy taxi distance of Rittenhouse Square.

It gave the management of the Pennsylvania Railroad fits. The inheritors of the proud traditions of aloofness and excellence established by Tom Scott and Alexander Johnston Cassatt were not reconciled to being also-rans in anybody's scheme of things, but the unpalatable truth of the matter was that *The Century* got the cream of the New York-Chicago traffic and *The Broadway*, at the time of which we write, got the race track touts, while there was barely sufficient patronage in and out of New York to fill half its six regularly assigned Pullmans. The Philadelphia Main Line aristocrats who boarded the Pullmans at Paoli scarcely compensated for the generally undistinguished *ton* of *The Broadway's* run of customers.

This deplorable state of affairs was commented on at length by Mr. Barriger in a memorandum to his superiors whose text is quoted in its entirety in the appendix of this volume. Elbert H. Gary and Myron Taylor, he reported, were riding *The Century* while the beautiful and costly *Broadway* Pullmans were being occupied by Madame Minnie Mandelbaum's Minstrels.

"Unquestionably," wrote the perceptive Mr. Barriger to his superiors in a memorandum dated January 5, 1926, "*The Twentieth Century Limited* is the finest name that can possibly be coined for a train and its natural appeal has been so magnified and exploited that the train which bears it has a remarkably powerful hold on the public imagination. Passengers almost feel that their own personal prestige is enhanced by using that train and that the extra fare is a social investment as well as a purchase of travel comforts and service."

To meet the competition of *The Century*, Mr. Barriger went on to suggest that the twenty hour service of *The Broadway*, which he hoped to have known in two words as *The Broad Way* to suggest the Pennsylvania's right of way rather than a theatrical district, should be supplemented by a fleet of similarly maintained twenty hour prestige trains run at various times of day so as to distribute the Pennsy service around the clock rather than on a single schedule and in direct competition in the matter of arrival and departure with *The Century*.

It took three years for Mr. Barriger's suggestions to become incorporated in the Pennsylvania scheme of things, at which time he was no longer with the railroad. In 1929, *Railway Age*, official spokesman for the industry, carried the following news report, showing that, as had been the case since the inaugural of the first twenty hour trains in 1893, the two carriers were still running drawbar-to-drawbar.

New Fast Trains Between New York and Chicago

The New York Central announces that, beginning September 29, it will run four twenty-hour trains daily from New York to Chicago and five from Chicago to New York, and that other trains will be quickened so that there will be three westbound and four eastbound (in addition to the above) which will make the run in 21 hours or less.

The Twentieth Century Limited, during the past year, has been operated as 2153 trains and has carried 240,000 passengers; equal nearly to three trains each way daily, and averaging 111 passengers to the train. Under the new arrangement there will be more regular trains and fewer second sections. *The Advance Twentieth Century Limited* will leave New York at 2 p.m.; the *Twentieth Century Limited* at 2:45 p.m. and the *Commodore Vanderbilt* at 4 p.m. *The Wolverine*, the present fast train which runs over the Michigan Central from Buffalo, leaving at 5:10 p.m. will be started at five o'clock, and will run through in 20 hours. Eastbound, these trains will leave Chicago at 11 a.m. (*Wolverine*); 12 noon, 12:40 p.m. and 2 p.m.; and in addition, the *Fast Mail* leaving Chicago at 9:50 a.m., will be run through in 20 hours. Altogether, the New York Central fleet between New York and Chicago will comprise 34 through Pullman trains.

The Pennsylvania announces that beginning September 29, it will have three twenty-hour trains each way daily between New York and Chicago. *The Broadway Limited*, now leaving New York at 1:55 will leave New York at 3 p.m.; *The Pennsylvania Limited*, leaving at 12:05 p.m. will leave at 2 p.m. and the new train, *The Golden Arrow*, will leave at 4 p.m., each running through in 20 hours. Each train will leave North Philadelphia one hour and 40 minutes later. Eastbound, a new train will leave Chicago at 9:50 a.m.; *The Broadway Limited* at 11:40 a.m. and *The Golden Arrow* at 2 p.m. *The Pennsylvania Limited*, now for the first time made a 20-hour train, has been running every day since November 19, 1881, or nearly 48 years. *The Broadway Limited* is 27 years old. The Pennsylvania operates eight other expresses daily between New York and Chicago westward, and seven eastward.

It turned out that the swing of public favor and patronage from The New York Central to the Pennsylvania that had been the objective of Mr. Barriger's proposals in 1926 didn't reach the exalted levels of *The Broadway* and *The Century* for more than thirty years and then it was by default on the part of the Central.

Ironically, by this time Mr. Barriger, always a devoted partisan of passenger service was no longer in the Pennsylvania camp, but allied to the New York Central as President of The Pittsburgh & Lake Erie, the harried Central's most profitable subsidiary. At the behest of Robert R. Young, by now the arbiter of the Central's destinies, its new president was Alfred E. Perlman, lately general manager of the Denver & Rio Grande Western where he had successfully overhauled the operations of that Colorado carrier from every possible angle except public relations. An expert engineer and exacting economist, Mr. Perlman's scrapping of many miles of historic narrow gauge tracks had not projected an entirely favorable image of the Rio Grande on the general public although he had beyond all question saved it from bankruptcy.

The year 1957 found Mr. Perlman giving the affairs of the Central much the same salutary but drastic treatment that had been effective in the case of the Rio Grande. Wholesale economies were being effected, not all of them with an eye to the best possible public relations, and what traditionalists feared would be the death blow to *The Century* was delivered in late summer. It was at this time that the various operating and accounting departments at 466 Lexington Avenue had completed their audits for the first quarter of the year and laid them on Mr. Perlman's desk. Whether by the instructions of the President of the carrier or in cold actuality, the figures for passenger losses, at least as there submitted for the forepart of 1957 were discouraging to an extent unforeseen by anyone who had been close to the actual operations for the period involved.

Mr. Perlman's immediate reaction was to insist that the deficit attributable by the accountant's figures to passenger service be brought down to manageable proportions but he recognized, and it was impressed upon him by worried subordinates, that the wholesale elimination of services would not be acceptable to the various commissions and government bodies involved and that to inaugurate them on an imprudent scale might bring about unfortunate consequences for the New York Central.

Among Mr. Perlman's moves was to consolidate the *Commodore Vanderbilt* and *The Century* into a single train, which automatically abolished *The Century's* long standing extra fare and incorporated into its consist coaches carrying non-Pullman passengers. There is no need to debate whether this declassing or downgrading of *The Century* achieved its immediate economic objectives. Certainly many of the amenities of niceness that had been its distinguishing feature over the years vanished.

Equally certainly *The Broadway*, which the Pennsylvania promptly promoted and advertised as the only all-Pullman run between New York and Chicago, was the immediate beneficiary and made the most of the opportunity to upgrade and restore every aspect of luxury service aboard its cars. Celebrities in substantial numbers began to forsake *The Century* for *The Broadway*. Two cars were soon added to the latter's normal consist and a little later, two more so that on days of peak travel it was a twenty-car all-Pullman flyer that would have warmed the heart of Alexander Johnston Cassatt. *The Broadway* piled up prestige for the Pennsylvania and profit, too, becoming one of the best paying passenger trains in the land and maintained in stylish livery and fine fittings accordingly.

Everything that Mr. Barriger had wanted for *The Broadway* came true, but it was thirty years too late to afford him satisfaction.

Few trains in the record have been able to evoke the loyalty and devoted regard that *The Century* has aroused in people not otherwise prone to abundant sentimentality. Arthur Dubin refers to

it unabashedly as "my beloved of all trains." Christopher Morley described the electric engine which powered the cars as far as Harmon as "the father who takes the bride up the aisle on his arm." "There are trains and trains," said *The Christian Science Monitor* editorially, "but no train has ever received such adulation as does *The Twentieth Century Limited.*" The author himself many years ago encountered at the now long vanished bar at Romano's in London an English Army officer of general rank who had only once been in America as a member of a purchasing commission during the 1914 war. The only things that remained impressed on his memory were Delmonico's Restaurant and *The Century*. "Riding it was the great experience of my life," he said quite literally with tears in his eyes.

Such fierce loyalty helps in part to explain the rage and anguish in the most unexpected quarters encountered by the Central management after the humiliation of *The Century* in 1957. People whose blood pressure would not have mounted at an affront to the Flag regarded its downgrading as a desecration transcending the destruction of Louvain by the Germans in the first war. The torrent of abuse and vilification that arrived in the mail at 466 Lexington Avenue horrified officials who had no idea they were tampering with what amounted in many quarters to an article of faith. The world of railroading was unutterably shocked.

Fanatic devotion has been characteristic of admirers of ocean liners and there have been partisans of the old *Mauretania*, the *Devonian*, the *De Grasse* and the *Queen Mary* whose eyes misted at mention of these incomparable vessels and who would travel on none other, but among railroad trains it has been nearly unique in the case of *The Century*.

The number of scrapbooks in which menus, ticket stubs and other fugitive souvenirs of a ride on *The Century* repose staggers the contemplation.

Happily the period of comparative disgrace suffered by The Proud Old Limited of E. B. White's poem was not of long duration. Whether the ghosts of long dead Vanderbilts thronged the midnight bedside of Mr. Perlman or more tangible factors were involved is not in the record, but after three years in the Central's doghouse, *The Century*, observers agreed, was being restored to a degree of managerial favor. By the end of 1961 it was once more clearly recognizable as a name train in the great tradition of railroading.

It still carried coaches and there was no extra fare but the Pullmans had assumed their spic and span dimensions of other days. Cut flowers achieved the profusion of an older time and fine linen reappeared in the diners. An office called Superintendent of Train Service supplanted the former train secretaries and its tenants were assiduous in their attentions to the passengers. There were orchid corsages and flasks of expensive perfume by Lanvin for the ladies and boutonnieres of prudent dimensions for men at the breakfast table. Club car attendants blossomed in new canary mess jackets with the insigne of the train in crimson sewed on their sleeves; cocktails and free hors d'oeuvres were again served with a flourish reminiscent of the Diamond Jim era and in place of the accustomed single morning paper, diner stewards handed the customers *The Times, The Herald Tribune* and *The Wall Street Journal.* The quality of the train's clientele immediately reflected the new order of things, and, as a final panache to the overall restoration, the red carpet, banished for the period of austerity, reappeared at Grand Central to make the departure of No. 25 the ceremonious institution in the life of a great city it had always been.

As *The Twentieth Century Limited* approached its sixtieth birthday in the spring of 1962, Mr. Perlman was also to contemplate its operation with something close associates felt to border on actual enthusiasm. It was grossing $15 per operational mile, which even with today's costs leaves a liberal margin of profit and the name of *The Century* once more fluttered pulses with the implications of excellence.

In recent years *The Century* has begun to turn up as a period reference to fix a date in gilt edge fiction like mentions of the College Inn in Chicago and Jack & Charlie's as a speakeasy. The opening scene which sets at once the mood and time for John O'Hara's novella "The Girl on the Baggage Truck" details the arrival aboard *The Century* in New York of a celebrated film star of the twenties. The photographers pose her on a baggage truck at the end of Track 34 with legs crossed and an inch or two of stocking showing above the knee. The vintage is as plainly 1926 as though it were printed on a bottle of Bollinger for that year.

As a coda to this brief survey of the train that has entered the folklore of the American people as surely as Buffalo Bill Cody, the Winchester rifle, mint juleps or the Model T Ford, it may be appropriate to quote an editorial from the *New York Evening World* for January 9, 1930, in which that by now almost forgotten paper was commenting on the naming of great trains.

"Of course," said the *Evening World,* "there is the name of names for anything pulled by the Iron Horse, a name so superb that one is almost tempted to say that after it there are no others. It was given that train of which The New York Central was so proud, and it is a name so magnificent that it should never be printed save in capital letters, thus:

THE TWENTIETH CENTURY LIMITED."

Direct competition to *The Century* on the New York-Chicago overnight run was advertised by the speed-minded Pennsylvania the same day of the inaugural of *The Century* in the form of *The Twenty Hour Special*, an all-Pullman extra fare flyer that met the twenty hour schedule of the opposition and ordered from Pullman luxury equipment that should not only rival, but if possible surpass that assigned to the Central's pride. In this rare action picture, *Twenty Hour Special* is getting into its stride in the late fall of 1905 at an hour in the afternoon when *The Century* was making tracks up the Hudson on its far less arduous scheduling.   (*Everett De Golyer Collection.*)

A high ranking Pennsylvania official, on a visit to Pullman, Illinois, was reportedly so fetched by a Presidential private train just outshopped to the order of Don Porfirio Diaz, dictator of Mexico *(above)* that he ordered a complete new set of *Pennsylvania Limiteds* including the beautiful cars *Veritas* and *London (below)* in an identical livery of green, cream and red, the Mexican national colors. *(Three Photos: Pullman Standard.)*

The changing vogue in auto taxis arriving at Penn Station, New York, are suggested here in two photographs from the collection of John Barriger. Above is circa 1910, below 1914, both are right hand drive.

The conductor of an older *Broadway Limited* and his engineer in a day before the antiseptic attire of Diesel compare watches before leaving Manhattan Transfer, New Jersey, in June 1924. (*Edwin P. Alexander Collection.*)

The departure from Chicago's suburban Englewood station on exactly split-second schedules afforded the dramatic view at the top of *The Broadway* and *The Century* racing on parallel tracks toward Gary, Indiana, in the early thirties. Not only does it depict the two most highly competitive name trains in the record actually running almost pilot-to-pilot, but it symbolizes the theatric quality of the intense rivalry between the Pennsylvania and the New York Central which, for six generations made railroading such a good show. (*John Barriger Collection.*)

The Pennsylvania Announces
THREE
20-hour Trains
to Chicago

Beginning September 29th, you can suit your own convenience!... Whether you wish to leave New York at 2–3– or 4 in the afternoon, you will find a Pennsylvania 20-hour train at your service ... And you will arrive in Chicago next morning at whatever hour is best for you—at 9–10—or 11.

The Pennsylvania Railroad has planned these revolutionary improvements in its New York-Chicago service, for the special accommodation of travelers from New York ... and in deference to the growing demand for fast, luxurious service at convenient hours of the day.

The three trains will be the Pennsylvania Limited, the Broadway Limited, and The Golden Arrow—and all three will conform to the same high standards of speed and luxury which patrons of The Broadway have enjoyed for over a quarter of a century ... No train offers a faster schedule than will these three between New York and Chicago.

For the return trip likewise, there will be three 20-hour Pennsylvania trains, leaving Chicago at 9.50 A. M.—12—2 P. M. and consisting of the Fast Mail, the Broadway Limited, and The Golden Arrow.

Other Improvements

Other important improvements in the Pennsylvania's service to Chicago will go into effect with the change from Daylight Saving Time, September 29th.

The Red Knight—new, popular "after-theatre" train to the West—will be quickened one hour—to a 20-hour 50-minute schedule. It will leave New York at 11.45 P. M.

The Manhattan Limited—leaving New York at 6.15 P. M.—will also furnish convenient 20-hour 50-minute service. Effective September 29th, there will be 11 Pennsylvania trains from New York to Chicago every day.

No Faster Schedules Than These

2 o'clock
PENNSYLVANIA LIMITED

The Pennsylvania Limited will lead the new daily procession of three 20-hour Pennsylvania trains to Chicago ... Famous for over 40 years as the first Limited train between New York and Chicago—the Pennsylvania Limited is luxuriously equipped—in every way a Leader.

Leaving at 2 o'clock in the afternoon—the Pennsylvania Limited will provide convenient 9 o'clock arrival in Chicago the next morning.

Westbound daily effective September 29

Leave New York	
Pennsylvania Station	2.00 P. M.
Hudson Terminal	1.50 P. M.
Leave North Philadelphia	3.40 P. M.
Arrive Chicago	9.00 A. M.

3 o'clock
BROADWAY LIMITED

Long the Leader of "the largest fleet of trains in America"—The Broadway's prestige—recognized by travelers for over a quarter of a century—will remain undiminished. For—though two Pennsylvania trains will equal its swift 20-hour schedule to Chicago—no train surpasses it!

Leaving at 3 o'clock in the afternoon, the Broadway Limited will arrive in Chicago at 10 o'clock the next morning.

Westbound daily effective September 29

Leave New York	
Pennsylvania Station	3.00 P. M.
Hudson Terminal	2.55 P. M.
Leave North Philadelphia	4.40 P. M.
Arrive Chicago	10.00 A. M.

4 o'clock
THE GOLDEN ARROW

Beginning September 29th, you can leave New York on The Golden Arrow at the close of the business day—and still be in Chicago by 11 A. M. the next morning!

This new Limited will be in every way worthy of its place in the Pennsylvania's "20-hour triumvirate"! Not only swift—it will be equipped with all those extra comforts which have made the Broadway Limited and the Pennsylvania Limited famous—observation car, club car, barber, valet, shower-baths, manicurist, stock quotations.

Westbound daily effective September 29

Leave New York	
Pennsylvania Station	4.00 P. M.
Hudson Terminal	3.55 P. M.
Leave North Philadelphia	5.40 P. M.
Arrive Chicago	11.00 A. M.

C. C. Trench, Assistant General Passenger Agent, Pennsylvania Station, New York, N. Y. For information telephone Pennsylvania 5600. For reservations telephone Pennsylvania 1100.

The Shortest Line to Chicago
PENNSYLVANIA RAILROAD

At all times during their competitive years, *The Broadway Limited* and *The Twentieth Century Limited* were breathing hotly down each other's necks in their bids for public attention, approbation and patronage. Much of the time the train consists were almost exactly similar: a combination mail and buffet-lounge car on the head end, Pullman Standard and later all-drawing room sleepers, fine diners and an observation lounge car at the end. Always they ran on exactly the same timing. But socially, until its twilight period for a short time after 1957, *The Century* was the prestige train on the New York-Chicago run,

operating in three sections where *The Broadway* had difficulty filling one. Above is *The Broadway* in the grand manner of American luxury limiteds behind a Class K-2s Pacific in 1912, showing its marked overall resemblance to the rival *Century*. Opposite is an insertion in *The New York Times* in 1928 announcing the Pennsylvania's adoption of the Barriger plan of three twenty hour trains to combat *The Century*. Below is a nostalgic period piece of old New York: the cab rank at Penn Station in 1910. *(Above: Everett De Golyer Collection; Opposite: John Barriger Collection.)*

RIVAL 20-HOUR TRAINS IN A DASH TO CHICAGO.

New York Central's 20th Century Limited Two Minutes Ahead at Rochester.

Pennsylvania Special a Minute Ahead of Schedule Time at Altoona.

Flying by mile-posts at the rate of seventy-six for every sixty seconds, engine No. 2980, eighty tons, of the New York Central, is rushing to Chicago, due in that city at 9.45 o'clock this morning, just twenty hours from New York.

It is the "Twentieth Century Limited," the new fast train, which yesterday afternoon at 2.45 o'clock pulled out of the Grand Central Station, and which in the future is to take the place of the famous Empire State Express as a spectacle, bringing the cities at least 100 miles nearer.

Among the notables aboard are John W. Gates and George B. Hopkins. There were other men of finance and trade and globe-trotters, officials of the road and newspaper correspondents.

The make-up included a combined buffet and smoking-car, library and baggage car, two Pullman sleepers with twelve sections, a drawing-room and a state room, and seven rooms, and an observation car. So great had been the rush for a seat on this, the first regular train to cover the 980 miles in twenty hours, that three days ago it was impossible to get accommodations aboard the flyer.

The train reached Albany at 5.32, Utica at 8.42 and Rochester at 10.10 P. M., two minutes ahead of time.

Passengers were taken aboard at all of these stations, but none whose destination was not Chicago. A hopper of coal was dropped into the engine's trailer, and it dashed onward again at increased speed after each stop.

The cars put on the new train yesterday were taken from the ones used in the Lake Shore Limited train, one of the star trains of the company.

When the train reaches Chicago it will be given three hours' rest and then it will start on its return trip back to New York, composed of four cars.

Martin Ryan, a tried engineer, was at the throttle of the big engine when the train pulled out of Grand Central Station yesterday.

The company follows the move adopted with the Empire State Express in having aboard a "resident" physician, in the person of Dr. John Reed.

Railroad officials and other interested spectators gathered in the Pennsylvania Railroad station in Jersey City yesterday afternoon to witness the start of the twenty-hour train between New York and Chicago.

The train, known as the Pennsylvania Special, was composed of a Pullman, combined smoking and baggage car, a dining car, a compartment car and a sleeping car.

It was just 2.13 o'clock when the train pulled out of the station, every seat occupied.

The only railroad official on the train when it left Jersey City was Mr. Barksdale, of the general passenger agent's office.

Another new train left yesterday over the Pennsylvania railroad. It was composed of four mail cars. This train has been added to the daily schedule, and will also make the run to Chicago in twenty hours. It left at 3.01 A. M.

The Pennsylvania Special arrived at Germantown Junction exactly on time, having run from Jersey City, a distance of eighty-five miles, in ninety-one minutes.

The flyer ran into the Harrisburg Union Station at 5.50 P. M. on schedule time. The run from Philadelphia to Harrisburg was made in one hour and fifty-five minutes. A stop of five minutes was made then to change engines and crews.

The train reached Altoona at 8.29 P. M., a minute ahead of schedule time. Between Cove and Duncannon four miles were covered in two minutes.

The direct and explicit competition afforded *The Century* by *The Broadway* had its beginnings in June 1902 when, with nice impartiality, *The New York World* for June 16 gave precisely equal space to the inaugural runs of the two trains. Down the decades the *Century* and *Broadway* ran neck and neck so far as operations were concerned, as is suggested at the right by Stan Repp's painting showing their simultaneous departure eastbound from Englewood, Illinois, in the day of open observation platforms. In the upper right hand corner of the page is a photograph of *The Broadway's* train gate at Penn Station, New York, taken by John Barriger whose passion for railroading extends even to taking his own pictures.

A chapter in the saga of rivalry between the Central and Pennsylvania's crack flyers and showpieces was written in 1938 when a new streamlined, all-Pullman, all-room *Century* designed by Henry Dreyfuss went into service at the same date of the inaugural of a new, streamlined, all-Pullman, all-room *Broadway Limited (left)* with decor by Raymond Loewy. *(Owen Davies Collection.)*

They all rode the cars of *The Century*: rich man, poor man on expense account, beggarman and thief, Roland Harriman soliciting funds for the Red Cross and Samuel Insull returning to jail. At the left are Madame Chanel who made perfumes, and below her, names that made society headlines: Mrs. Frank Vanderlip, Mrs. A. Barton Hepburn, Mrs. Harold Talbot, Dr. Alice Gregory and Mrs. Norman de R. Whitehouse. Jan Ignace Paderewski *(below)* like many other artists and musicians, felt *The Century* was his gentleman's club when away from home. *(Three Photos: New York Central.)*

Sailing lists on every section of *The Century* and *Advance Century* were kept as scrupulously as those on *The Queen Mary*, and, at the left, the Pullman conductor and train captain are shown doing their homework. Below: Madeleine Carroll and Lucius Beebe step off *Schuylkill Valley* at Grand Central returning from Hollywood where they had filmed "Cafe Society" which he had written and in which Miss Carroll was starred. (*Left: New York Central; Below: Associated Press.*)

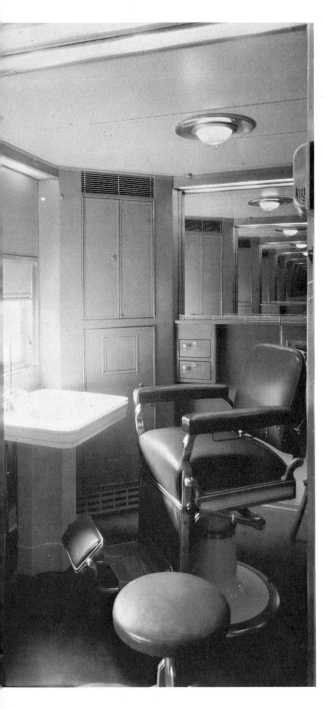

An antiseptic quality characterized the 1938 *Century* streamlined by Henry Dreyfuss that would have raised the hackles of long dead artisans in George M. Pullman's celebrated "Marquetry Room," but the barber shop was easy to maintain and the plain but stately club car rode on roller bearings in a manner that would have surprised bar patrons on such glories of the 1902 train as *Eudoxus* and *Proteus.* (Four Photos: New York Central.)

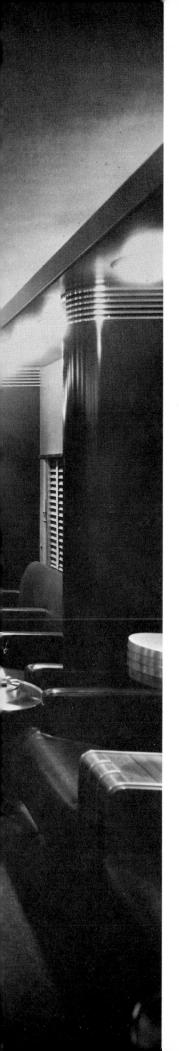

Gone from the 1938 train was the long accustomed open observation platform for photographing names that made news, but the head-end of the Dreyfuss *Century* possessed undeniable grandeur seen against the background of La Salle Street depot in Chicago and the skyline of The Loop.

The eastbound section of the Dreyfuss-styled *Century* was a thing of splendor in the morning sun as it rolled south out of Albany along the margins of the Hudson, well after daylight in the summer months. (*Above: Everett L. De Golyer, Jr. Collection; Below: Lucius Beebe.*)

The Century's diners as styled by Henry Dreyfuss were *moderne* and cheery and at the same time of ample dimensions for comfort. After the service of dinner in the evening a change of linen, lighting and music program transformed them into a conservative sort of night club without dancing. It was a period that saw the most intensive red carpet treatment of *The Century's* passengers at both ends of the run, the scene below being at Grand Central just before departure in 1941. *(Two Photos: New York Central.)*

The last fine flowering of steam along the banks of the Hudson saw the streamlined *Century* in a prophetic mood at Manitou with the Bear Mountain Bridge for background, drawn by the Dreyfuss J-3a Hudson type engine and pictured for immortality by Edward L. May. The equipment was, of course, Pullman-built and the best that money could buy. Patrons traveled in greater physical tranquility than ever before on any railroad, but there were old timers who lamented the beautiful dark green Standard sleepers and, most of all, mourned the departure of the open platform observation car that had for so long been the hallmark that identified a train of style and distinction everywhere in America. *(Above: Edward L. May; Opposite, Four Photos: New York Central.)*

One of the most camera shy trains in the record because of its hours of departure at both ends with resultant availability only in the long days of the year, *The Century* provided a rewarding photographic study along the storied banks of the Hudson whose margins it followed most of the run from New York to Albany. Here it is shown in a posture of sleek speed westbound just above Bear Mountain Bridge in the summer of 1940. On the page opposite, at the bottom, its rear markers are against a summer evening sky, still along Hudson water, and above as it arrives at Chicago on a winter morning to tax the capacity of the longest track in the trainshed at La Salle Station. (*Above: Edward L. May; Opposite, Top: Grahame Hardy Collection; Below: Rail Photo Service.*)

The photograph reproduced here shows Al Perlman some twenty years before he was to become President of New York Central while riding the road's crack train with a group of executives bound for Chicago. It was taken at Elkhart, prophetically, by John Barriger, a member of the group who was, in Perlman's administration, to become President of the Pittsburgh & Lake Erie, most solvent of the Central's subsidiary operations. *(John Barriger.)*

The long parade of motive power that had headed *The Twentieth Century Limited* out of the sooty train bays at Chicago's La Salle Station, beginning with the Lake Shore & Michigan Southern's immaculate Prairies ahead of four Pullmans and running through the tally of ten wheelers, Pacifics, Hudsons, Mohawks and Niagaras, came full circle in Diesel without style, distinction or claim to aesthetic attention, but utilitarian and economical beyond all their predecessors. Here the 1947 *Century,* drawn from a photograph in *Holiday* by artist Harlan Hiney, waits its highball at the now venerable La Salle Depot. For ironic background is a water tank dating from the times of steam which internal combustion finally supplanted.

Each section of *The Century* in 1962 carried, in addition to its conventional Pullman sleepers, an economy "Sleeper Coach" *(below)* leased from the Budd Company to provide private sleeping space at low-cost coach rates. Thus a one-way economy fare cost $48 as against a single Pullman bedroom of $50 in the extra fare days of the thirties.

Sixty years after its inaugural run, the two sections of *The Twentieth Century Limited* perform the immemorial rite of the meet in the darkness at Buffalo (*opposite*) while, dimly discernible at the left, is the ghostly outline of a water spout as a tangible reminder of the great days of steam. The up-to-the-minute galley still provides succulent viands, but not, alas, on the $1.50 dinner which once set *The Century* apart as a train for the affluent only. In the below frame is No. 26, still part of the long parade down the Hudson Valley of a spring morning, carrying the torch lighted long ago for "The Greatest Train in the World." (*Four Photos: New York Central.*)

Appendix

TWENTIETH CENTURY LIMITED

Changes in schedule

Train 25

Date	Lv. New York	Arr. Chicago	Elapsed Time
June 15, 1902	2:45 p.m.	9:45 a.m.	20 hrs.
June 1905	3:30 p.m.	8:30 a.m.	18 hrs.
Oct. 1907	3:30 p.m.	8:28 a.m.	17 hrs. 58 mins.
Dec. 1907	3:00 p.m.	9:28 a.m.	19 hrs. 28 mins.
Jan. 1908	3:00 p.m.	8:30 a.m.	18 hrs. 30 mins.
Apr. 1908	3:30 p.m.	8:30 a.m.	18 hrs.
Nov. 1910	4:00 p.m.	8:55 a.m.	17 hrs. 55 mins.
Nov. 1912	2:45 p.m.	9:45 a.m.	20 hrs.
Apr. 1932	3:00 p.m.	8:00 a.m.	18 hrs.
Apr. 1933	3:15 p.m.	8:00 a.m.	17 hrs. 45 mins.
Apr. 1935	4:00 p.m.	8:00 a.m.	17 hrs.
Sept. 1935	5:30 p.m.	9:00 a.m.	16 hrs. 30 mins.
June 1938	6:00 p.m.	9:00 a.m.	16 hrs.
Dec. 1942	5:30 p.m.	9:30 a.m.	17 hrs.
Apr. 1946	6:00 p.m.	9:00 a.m.	16 hrs.
Apr. 1952	6:00 p.m.	9:30 a.m.	16½ hrs.
Apr. 1953	6:00 p.m.	9:00 a.m.	16 hrs.
Apr. 1954	6:00 p.m.	8:45 a.m.	15 hrs. 45 mins.
Apr. 1958	6:00 p.m.	9:00 a.m.	16 hrs.

Time of arrival or departure shown in Daylight Time when it is in effect.

TWENTIETH CENTURY LIMITED

Changes in schedule

Train 26

Date	Lv. Chicago	Arr. New York	Elapsed Time
June 15, 1902	12:30 p.m.	9:30 a.m.	20 hrs.
June 1905	2:30 p.m.	9:30 a.m.	18 hrs.
Dec. 1907	1:00 p.m.	9:30 a.m.	19 hrs. 30 mins.
Jan. 1908	1:30 p.m.	9:30 a.m.	19 hrs.
Apr. 1908	2:30 p.m.	9:30 a.m.	18 hrs.
Nov. 1910	2:30 p.m.	9:25 a.m.	17 hrs. 55 mins.
Nov. 1912	12:40 p.m.	9:40 a.m.	20 hrs.
Apr. 1932	1:30 p.m.	8:30 a.m.	18 hrs.
Apr. 1933	1:15 p.m.	8:00 a.m.	17 hrs. 45 mins.
Apr. 1935	2:00 p.m.	8:00 a.m.	17 hrs.
Sept. 1935	3:30 p.m.	9:00 a.m.	16 hrs. 30 mins.
June 1938	4:00 p.m.	9:00 a.m.	16 hrs.
Dec. 1942	3:30 p.m.	9:30 a.m.	17 hrs.
Apr. 1946	4:30 p.m.	9:30 a.m.	16 hrs.
Apr. 1947	5:00 p.m.	9:30 a.m.	15 hrs. 30 mins.
Jan. 1951	4:45 p.m.	9:30 a.m.	15 hrs. 45 mins.
Apr. 1951	5:00 p.m.	9:30 a.m.	15 hrs. 30 mins.
June 1951	4:30 p.m.	9:30 a.m.	16 hrs.
Apr. 1952	4:00 p.m.	9:30 a.m.	16 hrs. 30 mins.
Apr. 1953	4:30 p.m.	9:30 a.m.	16 hrs.
Apr. 1954	5:00 p.m.	9:30 a.m.	15 hrs. 30 mins.
Apr. 1956	4:45 p.m.	9:30 a.m.	15 hrs. 45 mins.
Apr. 1958	4:30 p.m.	9:30 a.m.	16 hrs.

Time of arrival or departure shown in Daylight Time when it is in effect.

NEW YORK CENTRAL LINES

STEAM LOCOMOTIVES USED ON "TWENTIETH CENTURY" TRAINS
(1902 to 1935 inclusive)

Class New	Class Old	Date Built	Wheel Arrgt.	Road Numbers Original	Road Numbers Latest	Cost New	Tractive Effort	Length Over-All	Weight Engine	Weight Tender	Weight Total	Special Equipment
F-45	*F	1896	4-6-0	10-149	5020-5029	—	18160	56'-0¾"	118000	92300	210300	None
F-51	I	1899	4-6-0	600-610	5000-5010	$13400	24100	64'-9¾"	171600	126600	298200	"
F-52	I-1	1900	4-6-0	611-615	5011-5015	15825	24100	64'-4⅜"	172500	124500	297000	"
I-10	P	{1901-1907	4-4-2	{2900 Series Etc.	775-998	17300	23280	69'-5"	198000	130000	328000	"
J-40	J	{1901-1903	2-6-2	650-695	4650-4695	17800	25300	66'-8⅛"	186000	124500	310500	"
J-41	K	{1904-1906	2-6-2	—	4700-4734	18500	28600	72'-11⅞"	233000	159900	392900	"
K-2	—	{1907-1910	4-6-2	—	{3438-3594 4800-4894	20800	29160	78'-3¾"	273000	153200	426200	"
K-3	—	{1911-1923	4-6-2		{3267-3437 4895-4909	61400	30900	81'-5¼"	295500	207000	502500	Superheater, Booster, Train Control
J-1	—	{1927-1931	4-6-4	—	5200-5344	86060	42400	95'-11"	353000	306400	659400	Superheater, Booster, Feed Water Heater, Stoker, Valve Pilot, Train Control

*Added 9-20-38

Office—Engineer Motive Power,
New York, February 11, 1935.

From *The New York Times*, Monday, May 29, 1893

"THE EXPOSITION FLYER"

The Twenty-Hour Train for Chicago Starts On Its Initial Trip

Smoothly gliding out of the Grand Central Station yesterday afternoon at three o'clock, the New York Central's noted "Exposition Flyer" started on its first trip to Chicago. The compact train drawn by a mammoth locomotive skimmed over the track intent on making the fastest trip on record between this city and Chicago.

Six new sleeping cars of the very best type, two new buffet smokers, and two new dining cars have been constructed by the Wagner Palace Car Company specially for this service. There will be two of these trains almost constantly on the road between here and Chicago after tomorrow. Each train will consist of five vestibuled cars, tightly held together by Leonard's patented hydraulic buffer.

The cars taken out yesterday were the sleeping cars *Escort*, *Euterpe* and *Paoli* and the buffet smoker No. 62. The locomotive was the fleet No. 870, one of the largest and most powerful yet built. The cars were uncommonly attractive and luxurious, the polished dark woodwork and upholstering being particularly rich. The buffet car was provided with movable easy chairs, a writing desk and reading table. The buffet was well stocked with refreshments. The dining car was attached at Albany. There was a full complement of passengers on the train.

If no accident befalls this train it will reach Chicago this afternoon making the trip in exactly twenty hours. On some sections of the route the train will be run at the rate of seventy or eighty miles an hour, but the average rate of speed for the whole distance, including stops, will be a little less than fifty miles an hour.

John C. Yager, General Superintendent of the Wagner Palace Car Company will have charge of the "Flyer" on this particular trip. The passengers include a few railroad and newspapermen who make the trip as guests of the company. The accompanying picture of the "Flyer" is from a photograph taken on Friday when the train stopped for a moment at Croton Station on its trial trip to Poughkeepsie.

SYRACUSE, N.Y., May 28. The fleet journey of "The Exposition Flyer" through this state has thus far been in the nature of a triumphal march. At almost every station enthusiastic crowds greeted the train with hats, handkerchiefs and flags waved vigorously as the "Flyer" passed.

The ride along the Hudson up to Albany was a delightful one. The sun shone brightly on the placid waters and the air was clear and bracing. Standing in the open doorway of the rear car a passenger could scarcely realize the tremendous speed at which the train was moving. The cars were so firmly cemented together by Arthur Leonard's hydraulic buffer that they moved with but little vibration and no uncomfortable jerking or rocking. The steadiness of the train was particularly noticeable in the beautiful dining car where there was not sufficient oscillation to spill a full glass of water.

The run up to Poughkeepsie, seventy-three miles, was made in an hour and twenty-five minutes and the train reached Albany about six minutes ahead of time, making the trip in two hours and thirty-nine minutes. During the run the train on two occasions attained a speed of about eighty miles an hour.

At Albany the powerful engine No. 878 driven by the veteran Nat Reagan, gave way to No. 907, a machine of the same size. The train flew along to Utica with smoothness and celerity, reaching that city at 7:35 p.m., just five minutes ahead of time. The streets were crowded with people to see the train. The departure of the train from the Grand Central Station was signalled by the explosion of a score of torpedos, and it was witnessed by at least 2,000 people including President Chauncey M. Depew and Third Vice President H. Walter Webb.

Among the passengers are Col. William L. Strong, Arthur G. Leonard, Mr. Webb's private secretary; John C. Yager, General Superintendent of the Wagner Palace Car Company, William Buchanan, Superintendent of Motive Power, and J. R. Leonard, Assistant Superintendent of the Mohawk Division of the Central. E. J. Richards, Assistant General Passenger Agent, and Milton Reach, Eastern Passenger Agent, accompanied the party to Albany. The trip thus far has been regarded by the railroad men as remarkably successful.

Memorandum written January 5, 1926 by John Barriger in His Capacity of Traffic Inspector for The Pennsylvania Railroad To D. M. Shaeffer, Pennsylvania Manager of Mail and Express Transport, Recommending a Fleet of Pennsylvania Twenty Hour New York-Chicago Trains to Compete With *The Twentieth Century Limited*.

Item in box heading of *New York Evening Post*, Tuesday, December 29, 1925:

10 MILLIONS EARNED IN YEAR BY THE 20TH CENTURY LIMITED

Earnings of the *Twentieth Century Limited*, crack train of the New York Central Railroad, broke all records in 1925 with gross revenues exceeding $10,000,000, it was revealed in a preliminary estimate made public today, says the Associated Press.

The train which makes an overnight run between New York and Chicago was operated this year in almost 2000 sections.

It is the policy of both the Pennsylvania and the New York Central Railroads to stress the 20-hour New York Chicago service to the exclusion of other classes and to concentrate this business onto a single schedule on each road. Regardless of what may have been the supposed value of this policy to the Pennsylvania at the outset, it is working out to its detriment and should be modified.

Prior to the war, if my recollections and information are correct, the traffic on the 20-hour trains was very light. It was only during the strenuous years of 1918-1919-1920 that the increasing value of time, increasing average wealth and standards of living, and the relatively decreasing value of the dollar brought high extra fare trains from the realm of an occasional luxury to that of a general necessity.

From 1902 to 1918, the (eighteen and) twenty hour trains, while setting the standards of New York-Chicago passenger service were far from being the dominant factors in travel between those cities. Now they are. *The Twentieth Century Limited* was firmly established as the beneficiary of the new era in the utilization of de luxe service when the *Broad Way**

---

*Since *Broadway* refers to the Pennsylvania's magnificent line and not to Gotham's Gay White Way—is not *Broad Way* to be preferred to *Broadway*?

was restored and the advantages of the former were greatly reinforced through one of the most effective advertising campaigns ever carried on. Relatively little was done to exploit the *Broadway* except in Pennsylvania time tables and to refer rather generally to the System as the route of the *Broad Way Limited.*

Not very long ago, running the *Century* in two sections was an event upon the New York Central. It was only during 1921, I believe, that NYC 25 and 26 were placed upon a regular two-section basis, with a third section being required only during peak load periods. In January, 1922, the travel incident to the opening of the Automobile Show in Grand Central Palace, New York, required operation of the *Century* in five sections and it was an unparalleled occasion in New York Central annals which was featured long after in picture, story and advertisement. Now each day's *Century* out of New York and Chicago totals 20 or more sleepers and compartment cars and rush periods run the total from 30 to 50. While the *Broad Way* has been developing a substantial business, *The Century* has been developing a substantial business. *The Century* has been growing faster, both in actual numbers of passengers and in percentage of increase.

The reason for the latter unfortunate condition, which I do not think is as generally understood throughout the Pennsylvania as it should be, is that a continually increasing percentage of the New York-Chicago travelers are being educated to use only the 20-hour service and when this is accomplished, regardless of which road effected the result or enjoys the immediate benefit, *The Century* is in far the greater number of cases, the ultimate beneficiary.

Unquestionably the *20th Century Limited* is the finest name that can possibly be coined for a train, and its natural appeal has been so magnified and exploited that the train which bears it has a remarkably powerful hold upon public imagination. Passengers almost feel that their own personal prestige is enhanced by using that train and that the extra fare is a social investment as well as a purchase of travel comforts and service.

Aside from what seems to me to be an obvious and pressing necessity for the Pennsylvania to advertise the *Broad Way* on a national scale, it should overturn some traditional policies, which are strengthening its competitor at the expense of itself, by:

1. Not stressing the 20-hour service to the extent of confining service features to those trains.

2. Weaken the prestige of the *Century* among travelers preferring 20-hour service by forcing the splitting up of the traffic among other trains leaving at another period of the day.

Considering the above separately and in some detail:

Item No. 1. The difference in amounts of extra-fare between the 20 and 22-23-24 hour trains is small, if not actually trifling, yet the difference in service commanded by the extra fare in the two cases is tremendous. As service features are usually more desirable to the traveler than speed, he seeks the 20-hour trains far more because of their higher quality of equipment, service and comforts than because of their shorter schedules. The 20-hour trains are the only FIRST-CLASS trains from the service-equipment standpoint between New York and Chicago and they monopolize the patronage of nearly all passengers between those cities who can afford to pay an extra-fare and whose traveling convenience does not force the use of a train with a later hour of departure or arrival.

Both the PRR and the NYC are doing all they possibly can to focus the attention of the New York-Chicago traveling public on the 20-hour trains. The Pennsylvania probably assume that one of its patrons educated (or forced by service conditions) to the 20-hour trains will be retained by it. Unfortunately the grip of the *Twentieth Century* upon the public imagination is so great that a PRR patron who finally gives up the *Manhattan* or the *Pennsylvania Limited* for the *Broadway* is often soon lost to the *Century*. Quite a few cases of this have come to my attention, enough to permit me to generalize. While *Broadway* service, particularly equipment and dining car features, is superior to that of the *Century,* the difference is insufficient to counteract the lure of the latter's name.

The Pennsylvania Railroad should not exploit the 20-hour trains to the exclusion of 22-hour service. Our *Manhattan-Pennsylvania-Gotham Limiteds* attest to our ability to secure our share of the traffic in a field free from the pull of the *Century's* name.

The *Gotham-Pennsylvania-Manhattan Limiteds* should be counterparts of the *Broadway* from the service and equipment standpoints. I recognize the objections that can be raised to this, particularly extension of use of observation cars, inclusion of barbers and stenographers in train personnel, giving *Broadway* dining car service and the conclusion that the net effect will be zero (or a minus quantity owing to the expense) because the NYC will do likewise. I believe that giving 22-hour service of a character on a par with 20-hour service will keep a great deal of the traffic in a field where the Pennsylvania can control the situation rather than to force it over where they are at a disadvantage. We should do this notwithstanding the probability that the New York Central will immediately follow suit. We have real gains to be accomplished through the change. They will change entirely as a defense.

A second and perhaps more effective way of weakening the hold of the *Century* upon the traveling public will be to force the splitting up of the 20-hour traffic among several trains. The volume of traffic on the several sections of the *Century* and upon the *Broadway* certainly justifies, from the public's standpoint, the operation of 20-hour trains at more than one time of the day.

Basing my conclusion upon number of Pullman cars operated (with due allowance for 20-hour trains being operated on lower berth basis almost entirely) it is very conservative to say that as little as one-half of the total New York-Chicago business is handled by the *Century* and the *Broadway,* yet all the 20-hour trains (from 4 to 8 per day) have a single hour of departure and arrival. No effort is made to force all the 22-hour traffic and all the 28-hour non-extra fare traffic onto a single train schedule on each road, yet its volume is less than the 20-hour business and it certainly deserves no greater consideration in the important matter of range of choice of hours of departure.

The NYC under the present arrangement of concentrating all 20-hour business onto a single schedule on each road inevitably gets a larger share of the business than it could possibly have under any other so why doesn't the Pennsylvania force a new deal since it is within its power to do so. I know the objections to inaugurating another 20-hour New

York-Chicago train on the Pennsylvania but the game would be worth the candle. It would soon be operating on a very profitable basis and its business would not come, save in very small part, from other PRR trains but would be drawn from the Central. Remember the *Gotham Ltd.* Some thought that its establishment would merely mean dividing traffic of other PRR trains but how did it work out — No. 54's patrons came principally from Michigan Central No. 40 (The Transatlantic Limited). (In July 1922 I believe the MCRR's 22-hour New York train leaving Chicago at 8 P.M. had some other name and number.)

The present 20-hour New York-Chicago schedules are admirably arranged for those who do not come from or go beyond Chicago, but they are not well adapted to those making connections to or from the west. All of the most popular western limiteds leave Chicago in the evening and arrive in Chicago either in the early morning or (a few) in the evening. Thus, the large numbers of travelers between New York and western cities using these limiteds of western line in connection with the *Broadway* or the *Century* have longer layovers than they need or usually desire. The closest connections consistent with surety is the average passenger's preference.

The Pennsylvania has a greater advantage over the NYC in bidding for connecting line traffic at Chicago by reason

terests of the western and northwestern lines already there, except to a small extent with respect to Kansas City traffic upon which, however, the AT&SF has long had supreme control and the change could hardly take much business from the C&A, CB&Q, CMStP that they can get in the face of existing competitive conditions. All should benefit through the lighter financial burden of operating C U S through division among five instead of four proprietary interests and with the Santa Fe definitely taken care of, and hence out of any terminal project in the LaSalle-Dearborn-Grand Central section of Chicago, ambitious schemes, possibly overshadowing C U S, may have to be dropped or scaled down.

As an offset to the PRR's advantages in securing connecting line traffic, the New York Central using LaSalle Street Station "On the Loop" has the more convenient location from the standpoint of many Chicago passengers. While no rearrangement in schedules can deprive them of this advantage, a rearrangement can bring out the advantages of the PRR for connecting line business (particularly westbound) with corresponding detriment to the NYC. Schedules have never done this before — as eastern limiteds of both roads allowed such generous quantities of time for changing trains.

Arrival and departure at Chicago of principal limiteds of western roads are listed below:

Railroad	Limited	Arrives Chicago	Departs from Chicago	Destination
CB&Q	North Coast (NPRR)	9:25A	10:35A	Seattle
CB&Q	Oriental (GN)	7:55P	11:00P	Seattle
CB&Q	Chicago-Nebraska	7:55A	6:15P	Omaha
CB&Q	Denver	7:00A	11:30P	Denver
CB&Q	Minnesota	7:55A	6:30P	Minneapolis
CM&StP	Olympian	9:25A	11:00P	Tacoma-Seattle
CM&StP	Pioneer	8:35A	6:30P	ditto
C&NW	Overland	8:50A	8:00P	San Francisco
C&NW	Los Angeles	8:55A	8:10P	Los Angeles
C&NW	Portland	9:35A	10:15P	Portland
C&NW	North American	6:55A	6:30P	Minneapolis
C&NW	Northwestern	8:35A	10:00P	ditto
AT&SF	California	10:00A	8:00P	Los Angeles
AT&SF	Navajo	8:30A	9:45A	ditto
CRI&P	Golden State	10:00A	8:30P	Los Angeles-Santa Barbara
CRI&P	Rocky Mountain	4:15P	10:00A	Denver-Colorado Springs

of its being most advantageously situated with respect to the CB&Q, CM&StP, C&NW, and equally well located with respect to the CRI&P (by reason of Englewood Union Station). (Neither the PRR nor the NYC can be considered conveniently located to the AT&SF (using Dearborn Station) although the Central is the closer. (In this connection will the Santa Fe's efforts of some years ago, to enter the Chicago Union Station ever be revived.) It certainly should be a tremendous advantage to the Pennsylvania to have this great southwestern carrier housed with it, while not hurting the competitive in-

I believe that the Pennsylvania should establish a 20-hour train leaving New York at 11:00 P.M. and reaching Chicago at 6:00 P.M. or a few minutes before 6:00. A similar eastbound service should be established from Chicago but the time of departure does not suggest itself so definitely as in the case of the westbound train. The closer the connections with western limiteds the better for the PRR.

As to where the traffic is to come from, I believe that it will be largely from the New York Central and that it can be obtained.

From *The San Francisco Chronicle*, February 11, 1962

ON THE TRACK OF A DELIGHTFUL OLD LOVE AFFAIR

By Lucius Beebe

The thermometer outside Chicago's massive and venerable La Salle Depot said ten above and a cold sleet was placing a premium on what few taxis were running when I was set down a few days ago to take passage for New York aboard *The 20th Century Limited*.

The train shed was, if possible, colder and damper than outside and called to mind E. B. White's poem in the New Yorker back in the Thirties about *The Century* which began,

> *The storm king whistled out of the north*
> *As the crack old Limited started forth,*
> *With a hey, nonny nonny.*

It was more than half a decade since I had ridden *The Century* and the moment, renewing as it did an old love affair that had cooled, was fraught with the possibility of catastrophe.

For nearly three decades *The Century* had been an important part of my life, almost an article of spiritual faith, but when, in the mid-Fifties, it had incorporated coaches into its consist and ceased to be the all-Pullman glory that had ridden the rails of the New York Central since 1902, I had taken my business elsewhere.

The Broadway on the rival Pennsylvania had made a bold bid for the former but now disillusioned *Century* patrons. *The Broadway* was still all-Pullman, maintaining continuity with la belle epôque of rail travel through the agency of fingerbowls and fine linen, a top notch cuisine, cut flowers in the public apartments and the grand manner generally. My trade in recent years had gone to *The Broadway*.

There had been ugly rumors, too, about *The Century*—untidy service, no valet, downgraded equipment and the dimensions of second rate travel generally.

Of late, however, there had been other tidings. The management of the Central wanted to be in business again. *The Century* was being restored to at least vestigial traces of its older glamor; the management was giving flasks of Lanvin's "My Sin" and orchid corsages to lady patrons.

In a word, "the crack old Limited" of Mr. White's poem was striving for a comeback and I was agreeable to being shown. "Almost thou persuadest me," I had said to the ticket agent that sold me my space East. He had given me an uneasy look suggesting that I might be a refugee from Agnew.

And there in the train shed at La Salle, backed up to the train gate with the lighted legend of its name in the insigne of the observation car, was once more *The Twentieth Century Limited*, my *Century*, a train of such magnificence down the years that the management had unblushingly advertised it as "The Greatest Train in The World" with all the assurance that Rolls Royce simply says "The Finest Car in the World."

The streamlined gray Pullmans with the white finelining, 18 cars of them, reached beyond sight in the late afternoon gloom. On the adjacent track stood *The New England States* scheduled for half an hour earlier. I could detect no break in the continuity from where I had left off. Car tonks with torches were working in the brake rigging, at each doorway there stood the immaculate Pullman porter of old, the lights in the observation lounge shone with welcome. I was home again.

The equipment of *The Century* today is that of the new streamlined train of 1948 which had replaced the first streamlined cars and locomotives of the 1938 train designed by Henry Dreyfuss. The 1938 train had suffered grievously from the rough usage of a major war, and had been retired after only a decade, albeit a strenuous one. Until 1938, for 36 years since the train's first run in 1902, its equipment had been the last word in Pullman Standard of the time.

As of the year 1962 when *The Twentieth Century Limited* will celebrate its sixth decade of almost continuous operation (it was annulled briefly in 1919 during a coal strike), the differences in its over-all facade from the time your reporter last rode it are so microscopic as to be almost undiscernible.

Mostly they are visual: the equipment, more noticeably in the sleepers than in the cars of public assembly, could use a coat of paint and here and there the carpets are badly worn. Where paint has been restored in recent years it has not been the meticulous and painstaking work of the original builders and a particularly revolting shade of blue has been applied to the alternate doors to compartments in the corridor car I occupied. But in the matter of essential service, courtesy and operational practice, *The Century*, even to the most superficial eye, is an almost faultless train.

We left Chicago in the old manner on the precise second of 4:30, leaving *The New England States*, already half an hour off schedule, still standing on the adjacent track. It carried the business car of the superintendent of the Cleveland Division on its rear, and the high brass himself may have been late.

All along the Central and Rock Island yards to Englewood, flares were burning under the switches and car tonks were fussing with frozen brake rigging on equipment in the car yards. A mile out of Englewood we were doing 80, the ruling speed on the run, and the wheels had assumed the old familiar high pitched and sustained cadence of sound I have never associated with any other train or equipment. We were rolling, on the carding and undelayed by the calamities that might overtake lesser name trains, aloof and accelerated as a royal progress on roller bearing trucks.

The suburbs of Chicago, always a neon-lit leprosarium, yielded to the open hearth furnaces of Gary, looking like a preview of hell on a cold night, but the lake was still open and great ore ships were moored in the narrow waterways. At Gary the train superintendent of service and maitre d'hotel, the latter in a dinner jacket and the former in a blue and slightly rakish uniform, waited on me with a menu and took my order for dinner.

The superintendent of service is a function new to my experience and one that has replaced the old time train secretaries that made up sailing lists on *The Century* and attended to the communications needs of the passengers. Captains of finance, it seems, no longer give dictation in transit and the train no longer keeps a list of the names of all passengers on every sailing as was the custom for decades.

The two club cars, one adjacent to the diner and the other in the observation position at the end of the train, for all I could tell, haven't changed in their details in nearly a quarter of a century. Both were jammed at the cocktail hour so that I had one Martini standing in the forward oasis and then moved to the rear lounge where a single seat was available.

The Century has always been a drinking train, second only in its per capita consumption to the old *Merchants Limited,* on the New Haven, of which it was said the management could carry the passengers without charge on the profit made in its buffets.

As far as the eye could reach, *The Century* at seven in the evening was an undulant sea of Martinis, Manhattans, sours and highballs. Bottled cocktails conform to the now almost universal practice and I was alternately served Heubleins and Walker's Martinis, magnificently chilled in handsome glasses by bar stewards who could have walked out of the Pacific Union. Only their uniforms varied from the older and more conservative attire I remembered and now are bright, canary yellow linen jackets with *The Century* insigne sewn on their sleeves.

Twenty years ago I would have known a dozen people on any sailing of *The Century,* but tonight I looked in vain for the famous whiskers of Clarence Barron, for Arthur Brisbane or Charlie MacArthur or Ben Hecht or Damon Runyon or any of the old regulars. But where are the snows of yesteryear?

Dinner was more than adequate, but with prices half again as high as comparable items on the Southern Pacific, Santa Fe or any other Western road. There was grilled Lake Superior white fish, rack of lamb, shrimps Lorenzo and an entire page listing cuts of beef from prize steers purchased for *The Century* by Abe Smith, chief of its dining car services, from the 32nd Annual Junior Livestock Show at Detroit.

There was filet, sirloin, ribs au jus, the works, but at prices somewhat advanced from those when the train first went into service and established itself overnight as a prestige run by charging $1.50 for what on less exalted trains was the dollar dinner.

I slept the sleep of the unjust, awash with Hennessy three star and Upmann coronas as the long train rolled through the night over the widely advertised "Water Level Route."

Breakfast, achieved just as we came into Harmon to change engines for the electrified run into Manhattan, was the pattern of American breakfast under de luxe auspices everywhere with a menu featuring blueberry pancakes, Canadian bacon and a special hickory smoked ham that is Mr. Smith's pride. But something had been added from my memory; there were orchid corsages for women and tiny fresh boutonnieres for the gentlemen, and your choice, not of one newspaper, but of *The Herald Tribune, The Times* and *The Wall Street Journal.*

On the advertised and on the button, neither a split second early nor a fraction of a second late, we rolled to a stop in Track 34 at Grand Central. There were, contrary to malicious report, swarms of redcaps. There were courteous farewells, and come agains, from a solicitous train crew. If *The Century* has changed over the years in any material way the change is in the eye of the beholder. It all seemed to me like coming home.

◆━◆

Memorandum dated February 24, 1962 from John Barriger to the author detailing the operational changes of 1957-58

leading to the permanent combination of *The Twentieth Century Limited* and *The Commodore Vanderbilt.*

───────

Having made improvement of the passenger service, one of the planks on which he won control of the Central in June, 1954, Mr. Robert R. Young was naturally reluctant to curtail it and did so reluctantly only after unsuccessfully experimenting with new types of trains and other passenger service improvements. But by mid-1957 it was no less apparent to Mr. Young than to Mr. Perlman that a different approach was called for. The fiscal necessities of the Central required drastic and immediate action in order to reduce passenger losses wherever possible.

When Mr. Perlman came to the Central, its large fleet of passenger trains included three running between New York and Chicago on close headway and on virtually identical schedules. These were (1) the proud, de luxe, aristocratic extra-fare all-Pullman *Century,* (2) the all-Pullman but somewhat less proud, de luxe and aristocratic *Commodore Vanderbilt,* a non-extra fare train competing with the Pennsylvania's all-Pullman but non-extra fare (since Dec. 1942) *Broadway,* and finally, (3) the all-coach *Pacemaker.*

Even before 1957 there was insufficient patronage to support these three trains, with their full complement of cars consistent with the increased hauling capacity of the new Diesel locomotives. Consequently, first the number of regularly assigned cars began to decrease. Then *The Pacemaker* was discontinued as a single purpose (i.e. solid New York-Chicago coach) train and its coach service was provided by adding this class of equipment to the previously all-Pullman *Commodore.* (*The Pacemaker's* former name and number continued in use but in a service and on a schedule unrelated to its original purpose.)

The continued shrinkage of long distance rail travel under the impact of constantly improving air transport and new super-highways, together with the usual summer lull in business travel between Chicago and New York, so reduced patronage that separate schedules for *The Century* and *The Commodore* became unsupportable by July, 1957. Their combination, at least temporarily, was considered imperative by the management.

For four weeks from August 4 until September 3, 1957, *The Century* and *The Commodore* were combined. The timetables showed the names of both trains in one column, headed by the historic numbers of *The Century;* No. 25 westbound and No. 26 eastbound. *The Commodore's* familiar numbers, 66-67, temporarily disappeared.

Since *The Commodore* was not an extra fare train, the $5.00 service charge assessed on *The Century* was omitted while the two were run together in combination. When their separate operation was resumed on September 3, 1957, the extra fare on *The Century* was restored and it was raised to $7.50 on September 19, 1957.

In the timetable change of the following spring, 1958, the two trains were permanently combined, or perhaps it would be more accurate to say that the name of *The Commodore Vanderbilt,* trains Nos. 66-67, dropped out of the New York Central fleet, its coaches became a permanent part of *The Century* consist and the extra fare on Nos. 25-26 was discontinued.

Index

*denotes picture reference